# ANNE FRANK

## YOUNG DIARIST

By Ruth Ashby

**Aladdin Paperbacks**
New York   London   Toronto   Sydney

First Aladdin Paperbacks edition March 2005
Text copyright © 2005 by Ruth Ashby

ALADDIN PAPERBACKS
An imprint of Simon & Schuster
Children's Publishing Division
1230 Avenue of the Americas
New York, NY 10020

Designed by Lisa Vega
The text of this book was set in Aldine721 BT.
Printed in the United States of America
2  4  6  8  10  9  7  5  3  1
Library of Congress Control Number 2004107440
ISBN 1-4169-0606-1

# CONTENTS

# ANNE FRANK

## YOUNG DIARIST

# CHAPTER ONE
# A NEW HOME

It was a cold winter day in 1934. Bare gray branches stood out against the bright blue Amsterdam sky. Over a snowy bridge skipped a little girl in a short white fur coat. Her large green eyes darted about, taking in all the new sights.

This was Anne Frank's first visit to Holland, and everything seemed strange and new. Tall buildings loomed mysteriously over narrow cobblestone streets. Their steep roofs climbed up like staircases. Along the sidewalks, stalls sold steamy hot chocolate and spicy herring. On every street corner organ-grinders cranked out lively music.

Best of all were the frozen canals filled with

happy skaters. As Anne watched, a group of children all linked hands and swung around in a wide circle. A girl with long blond braids and a red hat skated at the end of the line. Faster and faster she flew—until she let go and swirled out across the ice.

Anne ran over to the side of the bridge to get a better look.

"Oops!" She bumped right into a red-faced boy with a pair of ice skates thrown over his shoulder.

The boy said something loudly in a strange language. Then he held out his hand to help her rise. Just then, her uncle Julius came running up.

"Watch where you're going, Anneliese," her uncle warned, laughing. "Thank you," he said to the boy. He caught Anne's mittened hand in his own.

Obediently Anne slowed down and trotted beside her uncle. But her thoughts raced ahead.

Soon she would see her father, mother, and big sister, Margot, again! Anne's family had moved from Germany to Holland a few months before, but four-year-old Anne had been left behind in Aachen, Germany, to stay with her grandmother Holländer. Anne could come when their new apartment was ready, her mother had promised her. Uncle Julius Holländer had volunteered to take Anne to Amsterdam. Then he would return to Aachen, where he lived with his mother and brother Walter.

Anne dearly loved her sweet grandmother, who always smelled like freshly baked bread. But she had missed her family. Especially her little kitten, Moortje!

The walk seemed to take forever. They entered a big triangular plaza surrounded by brand-new apartment buildings. Abruptly Julius came to a halt in front of one of the doors. He set down the suitcase he'd been carrying and pulled a card out of his overcoat pocket to read the address on it. "Thirty-seven Merwedeplein," he said. "This is it, Anne. Your new home."

Anne craned her neck to look up at the sandy-colored apartment building.

"Go ahead," Julius said. "Ring the bell."

Anne scrambled up the steps and pressed the buzzer. A minute later a pleasant-looking woman appeared at the doorway, her dark hair pulled back into a bun. "Mummy!" Anne cried, throwing herself into Edith Frank's arms.

They climbed the three flights to the apartment, Anne chatting all the way. "The train trip took forever, and then we caught a streetcar from the railroad station, and I had hot milk with anise in it . . ."

Her mother flung open the doors to the living room, and Anne went running in. It was filled with furniture she remembered from Germany. The steady *tick tock* of the tall dark grandfather clock made her feel right at home. Best of all, her favorite picture hung on the wall. It was a charcoal sketch of a mother cat with her two baby kittens.

Just then a small black cat scooted across the room. "Moortje!" Anne cried out, picking up the cat. "You've grown so much!" She burrowed her nose into its soft fur. "But where is Margot?" she asked, looking up.

Her mother smiled. "Since today is Margot's eighth birthday," she explained, "she and your father have gone out to buy treats for a birthday party."

Anne twirled around. "A party, a party!" she sang. Then she remembered something, and her face dropped. "But, Mummy, I have no birthday present for Margot."

Edith Frank hugged her daughter. "I have an idea, Anne," she said. "Margot doesn't know you're coming back today. It's a surprise. You can be her birthday present!"

"I know," Anne said excitedly. "I'll be a ballerina birthday present!" She began to jump up and down. "May I wear my tutu with the pink roses? May I?"

Edith nodded at Uncle Julius, who had come upstairs with the luggage. "I guess you can put Anne's suitcase on her bed," she said, laughing. "It looks as though I have a costume to find."

An hour later Anne was sitting on a table in the middle of the living room, all dressed up in her white ballet tutu. Brightly wrapped presents were piled high all around her. She squirmed in anticipation. When would they come?

Suddenly she heard the door open, and the sound of excited voices came from the front hall. "There's a surprise for you in the living room," she heard her mother say. An eight-year-old girl with short dark hair zipped around the corner.

"Happy Birthday, Margot!" Anne shouted, and held out her arms. Margot squealed and ran to hug her baby sister.

"There you are, Annelein!" Otto Frank, a tall man with a thin mustache, swept her off the table and into his arms. "We have missed you. Where have you been? Did you walk from Germany?"

Anne beamed at her father, who liked to tease her. She gave a happy sigh. She was home, and her loving family was all around her.

Later that night her father tucked her into bed. He pulled the cozy goose-down comforter up under her chin and kissed her good night. She could feel his mustache tickle her cheek.

"Tell me a story, Pim," she begged him. Pim was her special name for her father. "Tell me about the two Paulas."

He smiled and sat down on the bed. "Once upon a time," he began, "there were two little girls named Paula. One was a good Paula." His voice grew low and growly. "And one was a very bad Paula indeed."

Anne listened happily to the familiar words. The good Paula was sweet and obedient. She sat up straight at the table and finished all the food on her plate. She was kind to the cat and gave him a saucer of milk.

Bad Paula always fidgeted during dinner. She made a face when she had to eat her turnips. She pulled the cat's tail.

"Now, Anne," her father always finished, "who do you want to be? The good Paula or the bad Paula?"

"The good Paula!" Anne would crow, and snuggle under the covers.

Sometimes, though, she thought it might be fun to be the bad Paula for a change. She hated turnips too.

The next morning Anne's mother took her to see her father's new office. Anne knew that her father had started a business in Amsterdam called Opekta. It sold a product called pectin, made from ground-up apples. When cooks added the pectin to sugar and chopped-up fruit, the mixture thickened as it cooked. It turned into delicious jams and jellies.

The office was small and dark, crammed with boxes and desks. Otto Frank came out to greet them, smiling. "Come meet my staff," he told Anne.

"Miep," he said to a young woman with dark blond hair, "I'd like you to meet my younger daughter, Anneliese Marie. Anne, this is Miss Santrouschitz."

Anne curtsied, as her mother had taught her. The young woman had a round, friendly face and sparkling blue eyes. "Perhaps Anne would like to help me with the coffee and cake," she said in Dutch, holding her hand out to Anne.

Anne looked puzzled. "You'll have to speak to her in German," Mr. Frank told Miep.

"Anne hasn't learned any Dutch yet."

Miep repeated her offer, this time in German, and Anne followed her into the back kitchen. As Anne watched, Miep poured her a big glass of milk.

"Would you like to learn the Dutch word for milk?" Miep asked her, handing her the glass. "It's not too hard. Say '*melk*'!"

"*Melk*," Anne said, grinning. She took a small sip of milk.

"And this is a *moffen*," Miep said, handing her a cookie shaped like a little fat pig.

"*Moffen*," Anne repeated. "Oink! Oink!"

Miep laughed and continued making coffee. When they rejoined the others, her father introduced Anne to another one of his employees, a Mr. Victor Kugler. He nodded at Anne with a serious face.

While her parents had coffee in her father's private office, she gazed in wonder at the big black typewriter on Miep's desk. "Do you want to see how it works?" Miep asked her.

Anne nodded. Miep held the little girl's right index finger and brought it down on one of the typewriter keys. In a flash, a big black "A" appeared on the white sheet of paper. "Oh," Anne gasped. It was like magic!

Miep lifted Anne's finger again and pushed it down on another of the heavy keys. Another letter sprang onto the page—and another.

"There you are," Miep said when they had finished. "A-N-N-E F-R-A-N-K. Now you know how to spell your name."

That evening when Anne went home, she clutched the piece of paper in her hand. Every once in a while she glanced at it proudly. There was her name—and she had typed it all by herself!

The Franks were not the only new family in their neighborhood. Many Germans were fleeing to Holland in 1934. The year before, a man named Adolf Hitler had become head of the German government. His National Socialist German Workers' Party—called Nazis—believed that Germans were superior people, destined to rule the world. In addition Hitler told his people that all the troubles in Germany were the fault of the Jews. Germans had suffered defeat in the Great War in 1918 and a severe economic depression had followed. Many Germans were ready to blame somebody for their troubles, so they believed what Hitler was telling them.

Years before, Hitler had written in his book *Mein Kampf* (My Struggle) that Germany should get rid of all its Jewish citizens. Otto Frank, for one, took Hitler's threat seriously. Frank came from a Jewish banking family that had lived in Germany for centuries, and he did not want to leave his native land. But German Jews were beginning to lose their jobs and their businesses. So Otto and Edith decided to get out while they could. The Franks believed that in friendly, tolerant Holland, their family would be safe.

Anne, of course, understood nothing of all this. All she knew was that she had lost her old friends—and she wanted to make new ones!

Across from her apartment was a big empty plaza filled with sand. Someday this would be a park with grass and trees. But right now, it was one giant sandbox. When spring came, she and her mother went outside to the plaza every day. Other children were playing in the sand, digging tunnels and building sand castles. But they all spoke Dutch. Anne couldn't understand a word they said.

She was bored and lonely. *It's not fair,* she thought. *Margot gets to go to school. I want to go too!*

One day she trailed after her mother to the neighborhood bakery. A woman with a little girl about Anne's age entered right behind them. While her mother struggled to order some bread in Dutch, Anne wandered away to investigate the tulips in the window. They were so beautiful, white and red striped. She put her hand out to feel one. . . .

"Anneliese Marie," her mother said sharply in German. "Don't touch!" Anne jumped and pulled back her hand.

"Oh, you speak German too," the other woman exclaimed, her face lighting up. "We have just moved from Berlin, and live now on the Merwedeplein."

"What a coincidence," Mrs. Frank answered. "So do we." Soon they were chattering away in German.

Anne glanced over at the little girl, who was hiding behind her mother. She had a long, thin face, framed by soft brown hair pulled back on one side by a barrette. Suddenly Anne felt shy. She too moved over to her mother and leaned up against her long brown coat.

She wanted to talk to the little girl—but she didn't know what to say.

One morning in May, Anne put on a new checked dress with a crisp white Peter Pan collar. It was a very special day. A place for her had opened up in the local preschool—and today was her first day!

The school, a modern brick building, was a brisk ten-minute walk away. The teacher met Anne and her mother at the door of the classroom. "Hello, Anne," he greeted them, holding out his hand. "I am your teacher, Mr. van Gelder. Please come in. We've been waiting for you."

Anne peered into the busy classroom. Though it was alive with activity, everyone was quiet and orderly. Some children were sitting at tables and drawing. Others were building towers made of colored blocks. In one corner a group of friends bent over a book and giggled.

Her mother had told Anne that this was a Montessori school. Maria Montessori was a famous educator who believed that children should work at their own pace. Anne thought that was a great idea. This school looked like fun, not work. She couldn't wait to explore!

Around the room she wandered, her eyes bright with excitement. Here was a dollhouse, inhabited by little wooden dolls. In this corner was the library. In one cupboard she found musical instruments. She picked up one of the bells and rang it. *Ting-a-ling!* She was so fascinated, she didn't even notice when her mother left.

Mr. van Gelder came over to speak to her. "A friend of yours has just arrived," the teacher said, nodding his head toward the door. Anne looked up to see the little girl from the bakery. She looked scared and unhappy. Anne gave her a big grin and held the bell up for her to see. *Ting-a-ling!*

The girl smiled back—and dashed across the room to give Anne a big hug. "My name is Hanneli Goslar," she said in German.

"And mine is Anne Frank."

From that moment the two girls were the best of friends. They walked to school together during the week and played together on the weekends. When Hanneli wanted Anne to come outside, she stood on the sidewalk and whistled. No children on the Medeweplein ever used house bells. They were for the grown-ups.

No matter how hard she tried, Anne couldn't whistle at all. She would stick two fingers in her mouth, blow energetically—and nothing would happen! So instead, Anne made up her own little tune. When she wanted to call for a friend, she would lift up the mail slot in their front door and sing five notes: "La-la-la-la-la!"

At the sound of her voice, Hanneli—or perhaps Suzanne Lederman ("Sanne"), her other good friend—would come running downstairs. Sanne was quieter than Anne, with big violet eyes and dark braids. The three girls were always together. "Anne, Hanne, and Sanne" (Anna, Hannah, and Sannah) everyone called them.

With the other children, Anne played hide-and-seek and tag in the huge plaza in front of their apartments. They loved to roll their hoops along the sidewalk, whipping them along with small sticks. With chalk and small round stones they played *hinkelen,* a Dutch version of hopscotch.

Everyone in Amsterdam rode a bicycle. When the girls were five, they got small bikes with training wheels. By the time they were nine, their bicycles were big and black, just like those of the grown-ups.

On many Friday nights, the start of the Jewish Sabbath, the Franks would go to the Goslars' for dinner. Anne watched Mrs. Goslar light the Sabbath candles, a kerchief over her head. Afterward Mr. Goslar would pronounce the blessing over the kiddush cup. Otto Frank, not very religious, had never learned Hebrew. He listened very attentively to the prayers, but rarely went to synagogue himself. Anne knew they went to the Goslars' because her mother wanted to observe the Sabbath. Mrs. Frank and Margot went to synagogue every week. Anne usually stayed home with her father.

Year after year, on New Year's Eve, both families would gather at the Frank's for a party. Though she tried to stay up, halfway through the evening Anne would nod off and be tucked into bed with Hanneli. At midnight they were woken up for a delicious treat—Mrs. Frank's homemade jelly doughnuts.

In the summers Anne vacationed with the Goslars in a thatched guest cottage on the North Sea. Because the kitchen in the cottage served only vegetarian food, Anne and Hanneli named it the Tomato House.

Once, when they were eight years old, Hanneli's parents took them to an amusement park near the summer cottage. Back and forth the girls danced in front of the funhouse mirrors. First they looked tall; then they shrunk down. They had a wonderful time.

That evening a fierce thunderstorm shook the walls of the cottage. Terrified by the loud noise, Anne crawled into Hanneli's bed and started to cry. "I'm scared," she whimpered. "I want my father."

Hanneli held her shivering friend. "Don't worry," she comforted her. "The storm will be over soon." The next morning when she woke up, Anne couldn't remember why she had switched beds.

Year followed year, and Anne began to grow up. After a while, she spoke Dutch like a native. She almost forgot she had ever lived in Germany. Holland felt like home to her now.

CHAPTER TWO

# A GROWING DANGER

"You wouldn't dare, Anne Frank!" Hanneli whispered. It was 1939 and she and Anne were hiding behind the sheer summer drapes in the Franks' living room. "Think of the trouble you'll be in if you're caught!"

"You don't think I'd dare? Just watch me." Ten-year-old Anne took the cup of water she had filled in the apartment bathroom and balanced it on the windowsill. As her friend watched, wide-eyed, she leaned out the open window and tipped the cup over the sill. The water spilled out. . . .

And splashed onto a man standing three stories below! Startled, he glanced up to see where this sudden shower had come from.

"Duck!" Anne squealed, pulling Hanneli down onto the floor. "We're dead if he sees us!"

Breathlessly, she waited for the sound of the doorbell. It never came. Instead she heard her mother's voice.

"Margot! Anne! Hanneli," Mrs. Frank called out. "Time for lunch."

"We're saved!" Anne said, giggling. She and Hanneli crawled out from behind the drapes. Anne stood up and smoothed down her plaid skirt with her hands. "Coming, Mother," she called, winking at her friend.

Margot was already seated in the cheerful yellow kitchen, eating thick white bread and homemade cabbage soup. Anne pulled up a chair and reached for the bread. "Please pass the little mice," she asked her sister. That was what the Dutch called the chocolate bits they loved to eat with their rolls and pastry.

Margot passed her the bowl of chocolate. "Mother, when I rode my bike to the library this morning, there was a crowd of people at the newsstand," she said with a worried expression on her face. "Has something happened?"

Anne finished buttering her bread on both sides and sprinkled it with little mice. "Maybe the palace has announced that Princess Juliana is having another baby," she said hopefully. Anne was always interested in news about Holland's royal family.

Edith Frank poured Hanneli a big glass of milk. "No, this is news that need not concern you, Anne," she said firmly. "Now, have some more milk. I have a fresh strawberry tart for dessert."

Anne sighed. Her mother was always urging her to eat more. As if her skinny arms and legs were her fault!

"You might as well tell us," Anne said, pouting. "You know father will."

"Will what?" Otto Frank entered the kitchen, a newspaper rolled under his arm.

"Pim!" Anne jumped up and gave her father a big hug. "I thought you were at work!"

"In view of the news, I thought I'd better come home for lunch," Otto Frank said. He caught sight of his wife's disapproving face. "It's no use, Edith, they will find out anyway. The papers are full of it."

He unrolled his newspaper and held it up so all could see. Under the date, September 2, 1939, the headline read: GERMANY INVADES POLAND.

"But Hitler promised!" Margot exclaimed, in shock. "He told the English prime minister that Germany would not attack any more countries."

"This is not a man whose promises can be trusted," Mr. Frank said grimly. He ticked off countries on his fingers. "First Austria in 1938. Then Czechoslovakia last spring. Now, Poland."

"Do you think the French and English will stand up to them?" Margot asked. "Will they declare war on Germany?"

"Do you think Holland will go to war,

Pim?" Anne asked. Her gray-green eyes shone with excitement.

"Holland was neutral in the last war," Mr. Frank reminded them. "The queen has promised us that it will be neutral again. We shall be safe, you can be assured." He put down the newspaper.

"Father says that no Jews are safe while Hitler is in power," said Hanneli in a small voice.

"Hitler is a madman," Mr. Frank said, his normally calm voice rising a bit. "But Europe is a civilized place. He will not be able to get away with his despicable acts for long." He took a deep breath. "But enough of this," he said, changing the subject. "I think it is time for a song. Hanneli, do you remember the Chinese song I taught you when you were young? Didn't it go something like this?" He hummed a few bars in a nasal voice.

Hanneli and Anne giggled. They knew Mr.

Frank was just kidding them. The song wasn't really Chinese. But the nonsense words always made them laugh.

"Yin-yang, yin-yang, vosche-kai-da-vitschki," they sang loudly. "Yang-kai vi-di-vi, aya!"

"Really," Margot complained, holding her hands over her ears. "Mother, can't you make them stop?"

"That's all right, Miss Spoilsport," Anne said. "We were just going!" She and Hanneli ran off to Anne's room, still humming.

"Look, I've got some new photos I want to show you," she told Hanneli. Anne collected celebrity photos from movie magazines. "Here's Ginger Rogers and Fred Astaire in *Carefree*." She pointed to a picture of an elegant-looking man in formal wear dancing with a pretty blond woman in a long gauzy dress. "And here's Judy Garland."

"Who's that?" Hanneli asked, peering over her shoulder.

"The new star of *The Wizard of Oz*," Anne answered. "It's just opened in Hollywood. Look, I have the article."

"She's very pretty," Hanneli said, "but she looks awfully young."

"She's only seventeen," Anne replied. "Imagine being a teenage movie star." She tossed her wavy hair dramatically and patted the back of her head.

Hanneli made her fist into a make-believe microphone and thrust it in front of Anne's face. "What is the secret of your amazing success, Miss Frank?" she asked.

"How can you even ask?" Anne struck a glamorous pose. "I have a gorgeous face, perfect figure, and long, lovely hair." She gave her hair another fling.

"But do you have any special talents, Miss Frank?"

"I have talents galore. I can ice-skate, swim, and do hundreds of imitations. Here is my imitation of a hungry cat." Anne got down on all fours. "*Meooow*," she said, rubbing her head against Hanneli's legs.

"Don't be silly," Hanneli said, pushing her head away. "Real actresses don't imitate cats."

"Well, you never know," Anne said, getting up again. "One of the actors in *The Wizard of Oz* plays a lion!"

For the rest of the afternoon they pored through Anne's royalty scrapbook. She collected postcards of European monarchs, especially young people like Princess Elizabeth and Princess Margaret Rose of England, and Prince Carl Gustav of Sweden.

Her favorites, though, were their own good queen, Wilhelmina, and her daughter, Juliana. Wilhelmina had been Holland's queen for forty-two years. *Father is right,* Anne thought, looking at their queen's kind, sensible face. She would never let anything happen to her loyal subjects!

* ★ ★ ★

Eight months later, on May 10, 1940, Anne was awakened by a low rumbling sound. She put her pillow over her ears, hoping to drift back to sleep. But now she heard loud cracks, like far-off thunder.

A low murmur of voices came from the living room.

She tiptoed in to see her mother and Margo already up, still dressed in their pajamas. Her father was fiddling with the dials on the radio. "At four o'clock this morning German troops crossed the Dutch border," she heard the news announcer say. "Bombs are falling on airfields all over Holland."

Anne gasped. Holland was being invaded!

She ran over to her father, who put his arm around her. While her mother went into the kitchen to make coffee, Anne and Margot huddled on the couch and listened. They were joined by Grandma Holländer, who was living with them now. Her careworn face was tight with worry.

A few hours later Queen Wilhelmina addressed her people. Dutch troops were standing up to the invaders, she said. Everyone must stay calm.

The fighting was far from Amsterdam. Except for the dull boom of distant explosions, the city was quiet. Still, Anne and Margot did not go to school. No one knew what would happen next. That night Anne helped her parents tape the windows to protect against flying glass, in case the city was bombed. Over the tape they placed blackout paper. That way German bombers flying in the dark would not be guided by the lights from houses and shops.

The tiny Dutch army was no match for the might of Hitler's fighting machine. Three days later Queen Wilhelmina, her family, and the whole Dutch government fled by ship to England. Anne couldn't believe their queen would leave at such a time. She had deserted them!

Soon it was all over. The German bombs flattened the Old City of Rotterdam, and General Winkelman announced that the Dutch were surrendering. Holland had fallen.

The morning the Germans marched into Amsterdam, Anne, Margot, and their father watched from his office window. First came a procession of ironclad tanks and vehicles. Next came the troops, strutting to the beat of a military march. Row upon endless row, they filed by, their hobnail boots ringing on the cobblestones, their faces hard as granite.

Most Dutch stood in silent groups as the soldiers passed. A few, though, cheered the troops on. "Long live the Third Reich!" they called out. "*Heil* Hitler!"

Miep turned away in disgust. "Filthy Nazis," she hissed. "And the Dutch rats who support them."

"That's enough, girls," said Mr. Frank. "Come away, now."

Anne gave one last glance though the window. Across the street, a red, white, and black Nazi banner waved. In its center stood the dreaded symbol of Nazi might—the swastika.

For the next few weeks all of Amsterdam held its breath, waiting to see what would happen. When nothing did, life returned to normal, or almost normal. Anne and Margot went back to school, Otto to work. Edith Frank shopped and visited with friends from the synagogue. They almost grew accustomed to the sight of the German policemen, called the Green Police because of the color of their uniforms.

Anne knew that her parents tried to shield her as much as possible. But they couldn't keep her from finding out that the Germans had overrun Belgium and Luxembourg and pushed on into France. On June 23, Adolf Hitler posed for his picture in front of the Eiffel Tower in Paris. By summer 1940, the Nazis controlled Europe from Norway and Finland in the north, to Poland in the east, to Greece in the south, and to France in the west.

King Leopold III of Belgium was now in the hands of the Nazis. Thank goodness Queen Wilhelmina had escaped after all! Anne realized. Every evening the queen addressed the Dutch people on Radio Orange, the Dutch radio station broadcast from London. The Dutch must continue to fight against evil and not give up hope, she repeated. Good would prevail in the end.

Now Great Britain was fighting alone against the Nazis. Anne admired their fiery prime minister, Winston Churchill. "We shall fight on the beaches," she heard him declare on the British radio network, the BBC. "We shall fight on the landing grounds, we shall fight in the fields and in the streets, we shall fight in the hills. We shall never surrender."

Now, every night, Anne could hear the roar of the German planes, the Luftwaffe, on their way to bomb London.

Europe was an armed camp. It was almost impossible for anyone who was Jewish to travel from one country to another. That summer Anne could no longer visit her grandmother Frank in Basel, Switzerland. She could not go to the beach on the North Sea. Her mother told her that her uncles, Walter and Julius Holländer, had escaped from Germany and gone to America.

But for the Franks, the time for escape had passed.

# CHAPTER THREE

# "WHEN I GROW UP"

"Let me push the baby carriage for a while," Anne said to Hanneli. "It's my turn to be the mother."

It was late fall 1940, and the two girls were walking Hanneli's new baby sister, Gabi, along the banks of the Amstel River near their home. Orange and yellow leaves drifted down from the elm trees that lined the path.

"All right," said Hanneli, giving up the handles to Anne.

A cool breeze came up from the river. Anne bent over the carriage and tucked the pink wool blanket around Gabi's chin. Two tiny bright eyes gazed up at her. *She is so cute*, Anne thought.

She rolled the carriage down the path.

"How many babies do you want when you grow up?" Anne asked Hanneli.

"Lots and lots," Hanneli answered, kicking the leaves ahead of her. "Maybe ten. How about you?"

"I don't know yet. I want to be a mother, and do other things too."

"So do I," said Hanneli. "I want to be a history teacher or have a chocolate store."

"I think I want to be a writer."

Hanneli's new baby sister was one of two exciting things that happened that fall. The other was that Anne's father moved his office to a rambling old building along the Prinsengracht Canal. The office was so big that Anne and Hanneli would go there and call each other on the telephones. They wrote each other letters on the big black typewriters.

Anne had become good friends with Miep, the office manager. One day Miep told her the story of her life. She was born in Vienna, Austria, in 1909. After the Great War there were such bad food shortages that many people starved.

"I was so thin and sick that my parents decided to send me to Holland," Miep remembered. Dutch families had volunteered to help nurse Austrian children back to health. "When I was eleven, my mother put me on a train all by myself. I cried myself to sleep and woke up in Amsterdam. A strange man came to the train station and picked me up."

"Weren't you terrified?" Anne asked.

"I was too hungry and weak to be scared," Miep explained. "The man took me home with him. His wife gave me bread and cheese and hot Dutch cocoa. His children welcomed me as part of the family. Their love and comfort made me strong and healthy again."

"Did you ever return to Austria?"

"Only to visit. I still keep in touch with my real family. But I am Dutch now."

Miep's life was like something from a novel,

Anne thought. And now Miep had found her own storybook prince. She was going to marry a handsome Dutch man named Jan Gies.

The only problem was that she had never become a Dutch citizen. Her passport still said she was Austrian. When she went to get it renewed at the German consulate, the official hesitated.

Miep told the Franks what had happened next. "Our records show that you have refused to join the Nazi Girls' Club," the German official said coldly. "Your passport is no longer valid. Now you must return to Vienna!" And he stamped her passport with a big black "X"!

"I will never go back to Austria!" Miep declared to the Franks. Austria was part of Nazi Germany now. If she had to, she said, she would go into hiding and become an *onderduiker*—the Dutch word for "diver."

"Don't worry. We'll hide you," Anne reassured her friend.

Miep and Jan went ahead with their wedding plans. Once she was married, Miep would automatically become a Dutch citizen.

On July 16, 1941, the big day arrived. Anne dressed carefully in her best clothes—a pale gray princess coat with matching hat. She and her father would witness the wedding. Her mother had to remain at home with Margot and Grandma Holländer, who were both sick. Grandma Holländer had just had an operation for cancer.

Anne clung to her father's hand as they waited in city hall for Jan and Miep's names to be called. Other people from Opekta were there too. Hermann van Pels, her father's partner, cracked jokes while they were waiting.

The wedding couple looked pale and nervous. Jan, tall and blond, made a very handsome bridegroom. Miep was pretty in a dark suit and perky hat.

*But when I get married,* Anne thought, *I want*

*a long flowing white gown like the one my mother wore on her wedding day.*

"Jan Gies and Miep Santrouschitz," the clerk called out.

They stepped forward and handed the official their wedding license. "May I have the passport of the bride?" the clerk asked.

Slowly Miep handed him her passport—the one with the big black X on the third page. Anne held her breath. If the clerk glanced down and saw it, the wedding would be canceled—and Miep would be deported.

But the clerk didn't seem to notice. "It's fine," he said.

Now they could be married!

Ten minutes later the wedding ceremony took place in another room at city hall. Anne beamed as Jan placed a gold ring on Miep's finger. It was the most romantic moment she had ever seen.

*What must it be like to love someone so much*

*you want to spend the rest of your life with him?* she wondered.

The summer of 1941 was long and hot. The Nazis had passed a series of laws forbidding Jews to use swimming pools, beaches, or parks. Anne spent a lot of time sunning herself on the roof in back of their apartment. And she and Hanneli often walked through the streets by the Amstel River, pushing Gabi in her carriage.

One afternoon, after they had walked until they were hot and tired, they looked for a place to sit down. They wandered into a shady park and aimed for a bench where they had rested before. But when they got there, they saw there was a new sign on the bench:

FORBIDDEN FOR JEWS.

Suddenly the beautiful day was ruined. "What do they have against us?" Anne said angrily. "We're only children!"

# CHAPTER FOUR

# YELLOW FLOWERS, YELLOW STARS

It was getting harder and harder to be a Jew in Holland. Every month the Nazis in Holland passed a new set of anti-Jewish laws. By fall 1941, Anne and her family could no longer visit libraries, restaurants, theaters, gymnasiums, or zoos. She could not even attend her old school. The Germans didn't want Jewish and non-Jewish children playing or studying together.

Soon Anne was right at home in the new Jewish lyceum. Old friends like Ilse Wagner and Hanneli were in her seventh-grade class. She also made new friends, like Jacqueline van Maarsen, a half-French girl with curly brown hair and big blue eyes. During sleepovers at

Jacque's house, the two girls gossiped about the boys in their class. Jacque seemed a lot older and more sophisticated than Hanneli, who wasn't very interested in boys. Her old friend, Anne decided, was just too childish.

Suddenly Anne had a lot of admirers. Boys often asked to bicycle home with her. Anne loved the attention, but she set strict rules of behavior. Anyone who blew her a kiss or tried to hold her hand, she told Jacque, had gone too far!

At school, popular Anne could always be found in the center of a group of chattering classmates. Even during lectures, she passed notes and whispered to her friends. One day her math teacher, Mr. Keesing, had enough.

"Anne Frank," he said sternly, "you will write me a two-page essay on the subject of 'A Chatterbox.'"

*That's easy,* she thought. *It's a subject I know a lot about.*

*All women chatter*, she wrote in her essay that evening. But she had an added excuse. "I will try to control my talkativeness, but I may be a hopeless case," her essay read. "It seems to be an inherited trait. My mother chatters too, and after years of trying to stop, has given up the attempt. If she cannot control herself, how can I?"

Mr. Keesing roared with laughter when he read the essay. Yet Anne kept interrupting the class. A few days later, her math teacher was annoyed again.

He loomed above her desk in his gray suit and old-fashioned pointed white collar. "This time, Miss Frank, you will write me an essay entitled 'Quack, Quack, Quack, said Mrs. Quackenbush.'"

*What a silly title! Mr. Keesing couldn't really be terribly angry,* Anne thought. If he were, he'd have set her some extra geometry problems instead. She would answer a joke—with a joke!

The next day Mr. Keesing read her assignment out loud. It was a nonsense poem about a family of ducklings. The three baby ducklings are so noisy while the mother duck is away that they annoy the father swan—and he bites them to death. Mr. Keesing liked the poem so much, he showed it around the rest of the school.

And from then on, Anne was known as Mrs. Quackenbush.

She was always finding ways to entertain her classmates. Sometimes, during a particularly boring lecture, she dislocated her shoulder on purpose. Anne had a "trick shoulder" that popped in and out easily. It didn't hurt her—and it amazed her friends.

Or she would do her movie imitations. "Oh, Ashley," she would coo, batting her eyelashes like the actress Vivien Leigh in *Gone with the Wind*. "You know I will never love anyone but you."

Or she would lower her voice, like the

famous Swedish actress Greta Garbo, and declare, "I vant to be alone."

Of all the awful Nazi laws, the one she hated most was not being allowed to go to the movies or the theaters. It was so unfair to read about a movie in *Cinema & Theater* magazine, and not be able to see it herself.

To entertain themselves the Franks and other Jewish families organized musical evenings in one another's homes. Anne and Margot would sit on the floor in Sanne Lederman's living room and listen to a string quartet play the music of Beethoven and Mozart.

For Hanukkah the young people decided to put on a play, *The Princess with the Long Nose*. It was about a bossy, obnoxious princess who exasperated her whole kingdom. And Anne herself got to play the princess!

She threw herself into the role. On the pretend stage in a friend's living room, she strutted around the imaginary court. She mocked her ladies in waiting and disobeyed her parents. As she ordered everyone around she greedily stuffed herself with candy and cakes. By mistake, she gobbled down a magic cake—and her nose started to grow!

Frantically the princess tried to hide her grotesque nose. Finally she begged forgiveness from everyone she had wronged. "Good I will be and sweet as a rose," she promised. "Much better without this wretched nose."

The princess drank magic wine from the promised land, and her nose shrunk. She had learned her lesson.

A month later, Anne said a final farewell to Grandma Holländer. Her sweet grandmother was too good to die, Anne thought. She would always miss her.

It was April 1942, and tulips and daffodils bloomed gaily in flower stalls throughout Amsterdam. With spring also came another Nazi decree—all Jews had to wear yellow six-pointed stars on their clothes. The law had gone into effect in Germany the previous year. Now the Nazis enforced it in the rest of occupied Europe. The star was yellow, almost as large as Anne's hand, with the word *"Jood"*—Jew—printed on it in black letters. It was extremely ugly and humiliating.

"The star must be on all items of outdoor clothes," Mrs. Frank told her daughters as she sewed a cloth star on Anne's jacket. "Not just on coats but on dresses, too, if you wear them in public."

"At least it's so cool that I still need a jacket," twelve-year-old Anne said sulkily. "I don't want to ruin my dresses with that hideous color."

"They're like the badges Jews had to wear in Germany during the Middle Ages," Margot said, looking up from her book. Lately Margot had started wearing glasses. They made her look very grown-up and intelligent.

"Trust the Nazis to set the civilized world back five hundred years," Anne complained.

She heard Hanneli whistle two notes through the mail slot. "I've got to go," she told her mother. "We have a meeting of the club." Every week she, Hanneli, Jacque, Sanne Lederman, and Ilse Wagner met at the Wagners' house for some Ping-Pong. Originally they called their club the Little Dipper because they thought that the constellation had five stars. But when they discovered it actually had seven stars, they called it the Little Dipper Minus Two Club instead.

"Don't forget your jacket," Edith called out, holding out a tweed jacket with a new yellow star sewn right above the heart. Anne sighed and put it on, then rushed outside to join her friends.

They glanced quickly at one another's yellow stars, but no one said anything. It was impossible to be unhappy on such a beautiful day. As they strolled along arm in arm they noticed how new leaves had formed a canopy of green above their heads. In every garden plot tulips and daffodils grew. Even on the houseboats on the canals, window boxes were filled with brightly colored blossoms. All Amsterdam had gone flower mad.

"Look at all the yellow flowers in people's buttonholes," Anne said.

Hanneli pointed out a woman covered in daffodils. "She's wearing a whole garden in her hair," she giggled.

A tall Dutchman with blond hair passed by. "Good day, young ladies," he greeted them, raising his hat. Like them, he was wearing a yellow star on his jacket.

A group of teenagers from the local high school rode by on their bicycles and waved. Each of them had on a yellow star too.

Sanne turned to Anne. "Why are all these

people wearing yellow stars?" she asked in a whisper. "I don't think they're even Jewish."

Suddenly Anne realized what was happening. "The Dutch people are wearing yellow to disobey the new law," she exclaimed. "They want us to know they're on our side."

Amsterdam was standing up to the Nazis!

Anne felt a warm sense of pride in her country. "You'll see," she said to the others. "The Dutch won't desert us."

The rebellion, though, lasted only a few days before the Green Police cracked down. Protesters wearing yellow stars were beaten or sent to prison. Everyone was too scared of the Germans to defy them for long. The protest fizzled out.

Otto Frank refused to be discouraged, however. The British were no longer fighting the Germans alone—the Americans had joined the battle. When the Japanese bombed the naval base at Pearl Harbor, Hawaii, in December

1941, the United States had entered the war too. Now the Allied forces were fighting against Germany in Africa and Europe, and against the Japanese in the South Pacific.

"When those Yankee soldiers get here, Germany won't stand a chance," he told his daughters. "You'll see . . . the war will be over soon."

# CHAPTER FIVE

# *HARTELIJK GEFELICITEERD, ANNE!*

Early one Friday morning Anne woke up with a start. It was June 12—her thirteenth birthday! She glanced at the clock on the bedside table. It was only 6:00 A.M., far too early to disturb her parents. So she lounged in bed and dreamed of the day ahead. She already knew which birthday present she wanted most in the whole world. She had picked it out on a walk with her father days before.

They were browsing in the old bookshop on the corner of the Waalstraat. Otto was looking at English novels by Charles Dickens, one of his favorite authors. Anne was rereading a copy of *Joop ter Heul,* by Dutch writer Cissy van Marxveldt. It was a novel for teenagers about an adventurous girl and her group of friends. Then, tucked away in a corner with other stationery items and autograph books, she saw it—the most perfect little diary. It had a red-white-and-beige-checked cover and a small lock on the front.

"Look at this darling diary, Pim," she called to her father. She pulled him over to the display. "It would make a perfect birthday present for some fortunate girl, don't you think?" She tilted her head to one side and smiled at him while batting her lashes.

"I think I know what girl you mean," Otto Frank said, smiling down at his daughter. He loved to spoil her, Anne knew. She was sure the diary would be waiting for her on her birthday morning.

By seven o'clock Anne couldn't wait one minute longer. She dashed into her parents' room. "Come quickly," she urged. Bleary-eyed, they struggled into their dressing gowns.

Together they went into the living room. What a wonderful sight! Piled high on the big table in the middle of the room were bouquets of flowers and a heap of presents. As her family looked on, she tore open puzzles, books, chocolates, a game, and a letter from her grandmother in Switzerland. Her parents had given her a lovely blue blouse.

Just as she had hoped, there was her brand-new diary. "You're the best father in the whole world," she gushed to Otto Frank, kissing him on the forehead.

"*Hartelijk gefeliciteerd*, Anne," he told her. "Happy birthday!"

Anne set off for school with a basket containing sweet biscuits and a big platter of cookies she had baked herself. During the break she passed out the treats to all her teachers and friends. After school all five members of the Big Dipper Minus Two Club came to visit and give their presents. All in all, it was one of the best birthdays she'd ever had.

That evening, before Anne went to sleep, she wrote her first entry in her new diary. "I'm so glad I have you to talk to," she told the diary. "I want to be able to tell you everything!"

The celebration wasn't over yet. That Sunday afternoon Anne had her real party, for all of her friends. As a special treat Otto Frank had rented a projector and film. They watched the old silent movie *The Lighthouse Keeper*, starring the famous dog actor Rin Tin Tin. This time he rescued the daughter of a lighthouse keeper who was captured by some smugglers. When Rin Tin Tin caught the bad guy, all the guests cheered.

Anne wished Rin Tin Tin were her dog! She'd take him everywhere, even to school. She might need to be rescued herself someday.

For the next three weeks Anne settled down to study for final exams. She was a pretty good student in most of her subjects. The exception was algebra, for which she needed extra tutoring. The walk to the tutor's house was so long that she often asked Jacque to accompany her. They were no longer allowed to ride bicycles or take the streetcar.

"I don't dare do anything anymore," Jacque complained on the way home one day. The day was hot, and they felt sticky and tired. "I'm afraid that if I sit on a park bench, or shop in the wrong store, I'll be arrested and sent away."

"I've heard the stories too," Anne said. "Yet I don't know anybody who's actually been arrested, do you?"

"The British radio says that Jews in the rest of Europe are being sent east, to Poland," Jacque said stubbornly. "My father says we're next."

"*My* father says that there's no doubt the Germans are going to lose."

"Maybe. The question is, *when*."

"Oh, look," Anne said, changing the subject. "There's Rob, going into Oasis. Let's stop off for some ice cream. I'm positively famished." Oasis was one of the few ice-cream parlors in the city that was still permitted to serve Jewish customers.

Inside, they settled themselves on the red-leather counter stools. "Do you know that once Rob sent me a pin with a red stone from his father's store?" Anne whispered. "He signed it in French: *'D'un ami R.'* It broke after two weeks."

"Shhh!" Jacque said, poking her. "Don't look now, but he's heading our way."

"If we're lucky, he'll offer to treat."

A boy with red hair and a wide smile approached them. "Greetings, Anne," Rob said. "It's great to see you here. May I treat you to some ice cream?"

"I'd love some," Anne said, trying not to giggle. "May I present my friend Jacque? She likes ice cream too."

★　★　★　★

Every morning Anne had to make the long walk to school in the hot June weather. One day as she was passing the bike rack outside her apartment building, she was surprised to hear someone call out her name.

She recognized the boy as the cousin of one of her friends. "Anne," he began, "do you remember me? We met at Wilma's house a few days ago."

She looked at the good-looking boy with interest. "Yes, you're Helmuth Silberberg, aren't you?"

The boy blushed. "I hate the name Helmuth," he admitted. "My grandfather calls me Hello. I live right around the corner. I was wondering if I could walk you to school."

Anne was pleased. Blue-eyed Hello, already sixteen, was certainly a catch. "I'd be happy to walk to school with you," she answered politely, "since we're both going the same way."

She soon discovered that Hello was easy to talk to. All the way to school he told her about his life. He had left Germany all by himself when he was twelve, to join his grandparents in Amsterdam.

"I took the train from Germany," he told her, "and some SS officers asked to see my passport at the border. When they found out I was Jewish, they made me get off the train."

"How did you escape?" Anne asked, her eyes wide.

"Someone was making a fuss at the other end of the platform," he explained, "and they ran off to see what it was all about. While their backs were turned, I hopped back on the train. It was just good luck." He grew thoughtful. "That was in 1938, just after *Kristallnacht*."

Anne shivered. She knew about *Kristallnacht*, even though her parents hadn't told her much about it. On November 9–10, 1938, the Nazis went on a rampage against Jews and

60

Jewish property throughout Germany. Gangs burned synagogues and destroyed Jewish stores. So much glass was smashed in homes and storefronts that it was named the Night of Broken Glass, or Crystal Night.

"That name is a horrible understatement," she told him.

"I know," he agreed. "It wasn't just glass that was broken that night. People's lives were, too."

"What happened to your parents?" Anne asked. "Where are they now?"

"My father's clothing store was raided, but my father managed to escape to Belgium. My mother was caught by the Gestapo."

Anne gasped.

"It's all right," Hello assured her. "They let her go, and she found a truck that would smuggle her into Belgium as well. But I haven't seen either of them for four years."

Anne thought about how lucky she was.

No matter what happened, her father had told her, her family would always be together.

A few evenings later Hello came over to meet Mr. and Mrs. Frank. They made polite conversation over tea and cookies. Later, when Anne was in the kitchen clearing away the dishes, her mother whispered to her, "He is most suitable. Very nice and well mannered."

Anne raised her eyebrows. "I'm not going to marry him or anything, Mother."

"Of course not," Edith Frank answered with a knowing look. "He's just a beau."

Afterward Anne and Hello went out for a walk in the cool evening air. He was full of amusing stories. Once his teacher had tried to persuade everyone in his class to go to synagogue. Hello begged off, complaining that he had a headache. Later that day he ran into his teacher while he was roller-skating!

Then there was the time he turned thirteen and had his bar mitzvah, his coming of age ceremony, in the local synagogue. The top hat was so large for him that his grandmother had to stuff newspaper in it to keep it on his head.

"The whole time I was reciting the Torah, I had to hold my head very still," Hello remembered. "Then, when I was finished, the rabbi put his hand on my head to give me the blessing. The hat slipped over my eyes and I couldn't see a thing!"

Anne roared with laughter. She was enjoying herself so much that she forgot about the time. At ten minutes after eight she came in the front door of her apartment and found her father pacing back and forth in the living room.

"I am very disappointed in you, Anne," Otto Frank snapped at her. "You know how dangerous it is to stay out past the eight o'clock curfew. Who knows what might happen if you were caught by the Green Police!"

Anne's good mood was gone in an instant. It was frightening to see her usually calm father so angry. "I am so sorry, Pim," she said, hanging her head. "I will never be late again. Really, I promise."

"From now on, be in by ten to eight," Otto Frank ordered her. He gave her a big hug. "Now go and see your mother. She is worried sick about you."

That Friday, July 3, Anne graduated from the seventh grade with the rest of her class. She had done fairly well in most of her subjects. Only in her hated algebra class did she earn a C-. Margot, as usual, had graduated with honors.

As she watched her friends walk up to the podium to get their diplomas, Anne's mind drifted back to a conversation she had had with her father the day before.

She and Otto Frank were taking a walk around the block when he brought the subject up. "I'm sure you've noticed, Anne, that some of our furniture and other belongings have been disappearing."

Anne frowned. "I thought they were being sent out for repair," she replied.

"Actually," her father said, "we have been sending them to a place the Germans can't find them." He paused. "We may also have to leave and go someplace the Germans can't find *us*."

Anne felt her heart stop. "You mean we'll be leaving Amsterdam, Father?" she said in disbelief. "But when?"

Otto Frank smiled and put his arm around his daughter. "Never mind that. Just enjoy yourself this summer and let me worry about the future."

Anne hoped that this particular future was a very long time away.

# INTO HIDING

Sunday, July 5, was a lovely summer day. The sun shone brightly in a pure blue sky, studded with fat white clouds. It was, Anne thought, the perfect beginning to summer vacation. She slipped into some shorts and a sleeveless top, eager to get a tan.

Hello stopped by in the morning, and they sat outside on the kitchen balcony, chatting and soaking up the sun. After he went home for lunch, she stayed outside reading a book. He would come back later, Hello promised. Maybe they could take a walk.

The lazy afternoon drifted by. Then, at about three o'clock, the doorbell rang.

A few minutes later Margot came out on the

balcony. As soon as she saw her, Anne could tell something was terribly wrong.

"The most awful thing has happened," Margot exclaimed. Her usually pale face was flushed, and she looked as if on the verge of tears. "Mother has just opened a letter from the German SS. Father has received a call-up notice!"

Anne felt her body go cold with fright. A call-up notice? She knew what that meant. Just as Jacque had warned, Jews in Amsterdam were being taken in *razias,* the Dutch word for roundup. The Germans said they were being shipped to labor camps. But who knew where they were really going?

How could her father, her beloved Pim, be taken away from them? She wanted to run to him to be comforted. Yet she knew he was not even home. Otto Frank was out for the afternoon, visiting some friends at the Jewish old people's home.

Anne began to cry. "He can't go, he just can't," she repeated. "Oh, what are we going to do?" She got up and stumbled through the door, in search of her mother.

"Mother's gone to find Mr. van Pels," said Margot, following Anne back into the house. "We're going to go into hiding immediately, maybe tomorrow. The van Pels are going to join us there."

Speechless, Anne just stared at her sister. Hiding? So soon? A million thoughts and questions shot through her head, but she said nothing. She tumbled onto a couch to wait. Margot sat down opposite her.

The minutes ticked by.

*Buzz!* The doorbell rang. "Don't answer it," Margot commanded.

"But what if it's Hello?" Anne said. "He said he'd come back."

"Mother said not to answer the door for anybody."

The bell rang again. Poor Hello, Anne thought. He must wonder what's happened to us.

Later she heard the apartment door open. Edith Frank came in, followed by Hermann van Pels, her father's business partner. Anne stood up, ready to shoot off her questions. Yet when she saw her mother's face, she stopped. It had a white, pinched look that Anne had never seen before.

"Mr. van Pels and I have many things to discuss," Edith said in a flat voice. "You girls go into your room and begin to pack. Take only what is necessary." Her voice broke. "Please, go. And don't worry. Your father will be home soon."

Moortje, their cat, was curled up on Anne's bed. Gathering her pet in her arms, Anne buried her face in his fur.

"Anne, I have a confession to make," she heard Margot murmur from the other bed.

"It's not Father who's been called up. It's me."

Anne whirled to face her sister. "How can that be?" she cried. "You're only sixteen! Why would they take teenagers from their families? Why?" She started to sob again, tears racking her body.

"It's not going to happen," Margot said, her lip trembling. "Mother and Father said that we will not be separated, no matter what."

The two girls looked at each other in silence. "Come on," Margot said finally. "Let's get packing."

Anne took out her schoolbag and started to cram in her belongings. Her new diary went in first, of course. Then hair curlers, books, photos, letters, cold cream, a toothbrush, a comb. *Maybe I should be bringing more clothes,* she worried. But family mementos seemed much more important at a time like this.

Early that evening Otto Frank finally arrived home. Immediately he took charge, as

Anne knew he would. Yes, they would go into hiding the very next morning, he told them calmly. First he would call Mr. Kleiman from the office and ask him to stop by. Then Mr. van Pels would go fetch Miep and Jan Gies to help take away their things. In the meantime they would all get ready.

"But Pim," Anne said, clinging to his arm. "Where are we going? To another city? To another country? To Switzerland, to be with Grandmother? Or to England?"

"Hush," Otto Frank said gently. "We made our plans long ago. You will find out the specifics in due time. Now help us."

The night crept by like a bad dream. With their mother, Anne and Margot sorted through endless piles of clothes—sweaters, skirts, blouses, stockings, handkerchiefs, shoes, many sets of underwear, a combing shawl. Edith handed them over to Miep Gies, who stuffed whatever she could into her bag and the pockets of her old raincoat. Then came more sorting, until Miep and Jan appeared again and took more belongings out into the night.

Shortly after midnight Anne crawled into bed, utterly exhausted. She barely had time to think *This is the last night I'll spend in my own house* when she fell fast asleep.

"Anne, wake up," her mother said, shaking her gently. Anne opened her eyes and was wide awake in an instant. *Today is the day we're going into hiding,* she thought.

They had a hurried breakfast, then rushed around taking care of last-minute details. Otto Frank wrote a quick note to his sister, Helene, who lived with his mother in Basel, Switzerland. He did not dare tell her what his family was doing. But he let her know they would all stay together.

Anne begged to be able to add a message at the end. "I will not be able to write you a holiday letter now," she scribbled. Would her aunt and grandmother be able to read between the lines? Would they understand that she would write if she could?

Otto Frank also left a slip of paper on his desk on which he had jotted the name of a town on the Swiss border. He wanted the authorities to think that the family had escaped to Switzerland. Then they wouldn't search for them here in Amsterdam.

Before 7:30 Miep arrived at the door to pick up Margot. Together they would ride their bicycles to the hiding place. "But what about the Green Police?" Anne asked anxiously. "It is illegal for Margot to be seen riding a bicycle."

"Not even the Green Police will be out on a day like this," Miep assured her. Outside, it was raining hard. "We will look like two very wet working girls on our way to the office."

Off they pedaled in the downpour. Anne piled on as many layers of clothing as she could—two pairs of stockings, two undershirts and two pairs of underpants, a dress, a shirt, a sweater, and more. Over it all she threw on her raincoat, with its bright yellow star.

Mrs. Frank left a pound of meat for Moortje and a note asking their lodger, Mr. Goldschmidt, to take the cat to a neighbor's home for safe-keeping. They could not take her with them, she explained to Anne. A cat would draw too much attention to their hiding place.

"Good-bye, my Moortje," Anne cooed, stroking the cat. Moortje gave a soft *meow* and rubbed her head against Anne's hand. "Don't worry, we will return for you soon. In just a few weeks or months, I hope. You will be well fed while we are gone."

Her mother touched her arm to motion her out. As they left the apartment Anne turned her head to look back at the kitchen. For the first time she could remember, her mother had left the breakfast plates still on the table.

Already Moortje was nosing about for scraps of food.

Then they were down the stairs and out on the Amsterdam streets in the teeming rain.

They had left without any luggage, since carrying suitcases would have been suspicious. Instead, Anne and her parents were each lugging a schoolbag and shopping bag. The walk seemed to take forever, down wide boulevards, over busy bridges, and through narrow cobblestone alleys. Some of the passersby looked at them sympathetically, as if they would help them if they could. But Christians were forbidden to talk to Jews, and Jews were forbidden to ride streetcars.

Finally, drenched and perspiring under their many layers of clothes, they turned onto a very familiar street. It was the Prinsengracht!

"Father, this is the way to your office," Anne said in wonder.

"You have guessed the mystery," her father

explained. "That is where we shall be hiding. Behind the regular office there is another set of rooms. It is a secret annex, invisible from the street. Only the office staff will know that we are there. They will be our helpers."

Miep had arrived earlier with Margot and was waiting for them. Quickly she guided them through the front office, a crowded alcove, and a dark back office, then up a staircase to the third floor. They made a quick turn to the right, climbed up one small step, and passed through a small gray door. Anne had a quick glimpse of a dark hall and a steep flight of stairs. Then the door shut behind them.

This was it, then. The Secret Annex.

# CHAPTER SEVEN

# THE SECRET ANNEX

Curious, Anne stepped into the first small room. *This place is a mess,* she realized, looking around. Cardboard boxes, furniture, pots, pans, and bed linens were heaped everywhere. Sitting on one small bed in the corner was Margot, looking pale and forlorn. She had been waiting for hours for them to arrive.

Edith Frank collapsed next to Margot and put her arm around her daughter's shoulder. "I don't think I can take another step," she said in a faint voice.

Otto Frank looked at his wife with concern. "You rest, Edith, and I'll show the girls around." He held out his hand for Margot and pulled her up. "This will be our room, your mother's and mine." It was a small room, only about seventeen feet by ten feet, with green paneling halfway up the wall. At one end was a big window looking out onto a back garden.

"And here," her father continued, stepping into an adjoining room, "is your bedroom, Anne, which you and Margot will share."

Hastily Anne threw off her raincoat and sweater and followed him in. This room was even narrower than the first, no wider than the window at the far end. It also had green paneling and faded orange-colored wallpaper.

"This could certainly use some cheering up," Anne commented. She went over to the window and peered out. Through the thick leaves of a chestnut tree, she could see a sparrow perched on a branch.

"Stay away from the window," her father said urgently. "We don't want any nosy neighbors to see us."

Startled, Anne jumped away. She followed

her father into the bathroom, which had another door onto the hall. "You can thank Mr. Kleiman for this toilet and wash basin," Mr. Frank explained. "He installed them just a month ago."

Margot found her voice. "Is there just one bathroom for all of us?"

"I'm afraid so, my dear." He winked at Anne. "You young ladies will have to use your time wisely. No more spending hours in front of the mirror."

Anne made a face at him. It was good to hear her father tease her again.

Finally they clambered up the steep stairs to the next floor. At the top sat a large, light room with a stove and sink. This would be their common area—their kitchen and living room—and Mr. and Mrs. van Pels's bedroom all rolled into one. Off this room was a tiny cubbyhole with a ladder leading up to the attic. Peter van Pels, their teenage son, would have the cubbyhole all to himself.

Exhausted, Margot joined her mother for a nap. Anne, though, was full of nervous energy. When her father suggested they start cleaning up, she was happy to join in.

First they sewed curtains from scraps of fabric and tacked them over the windows. That way, no prying eyes could see in. At night Mr. Frank would put up thick blackout cardboard as well, to keep the light from escaping.

Then they swept and scrubbed, unrolled carpets and made the beds. Anne unpacked boxes of plates, saucers, and cups, stacking them neatly in the white cupboards in the common room. The big table in the middle of the room was surrounded by the oddest assortment of chairs Anne had ever seen. She was amazed to recognize some of them as old Frank family chairs that had mysteriously vanished many months before. Together she and her father fastened a ceiling lamp with a fringed shade over the middle of the table. It cast a warm light over the room.

The next day, as she and Margot were folding their clothes and putting them in cupboards, Otto Frank came into their room with a carton. "Guess what I found," he said with a grin, handing the box to Anne. She glanced in—and saw her whole collection of movie star pictures and royalty postcards! She threw her arms around her father. "You always think of everything," she said, beaming. Trust her beloved Pim to remember her special pictures.

"And here is some glue," he added, holding out a pot and a brush. "Why not paste them on your walls?"

Up went her photographs of movie stars Greta Garbo, Ray Milland, Ginger Rogers, and the Dutch actress Lily Bouwmeester. She added other special picture favorites: Princesses Elizabeth and Margaret Rose of England, Michelangelo's *Pieta,* the head of the Greek god

Apollo, a bunch of cute babies, the Goslars' thatched summer cottage, chimpanzees having a tea party, and lots more. Soon the whole wall next to her bed was covered with pictures.

"Now it looks more homelike," she announced to Margot.

Not until Wednesday did she steal a moment to write in her diary. She recorded everything that had happened in the last three days.

She felt as if her whole world had turned upside down. And who knew what changes were yet to come?

On July 13, the Van Pels family arrived. Fifteen-year-old Peter came first, right in the middle of breakfast. He stood in the doorway, clutching a backpack in his hand and looking uncertain.

Otto Frank stood up. "Welcome," he said, extending his hand. "We are glad to have you with us."

Peter put the backpack down—and Anne

heard a loud mewing sound from inside. She hopped off her chair and unbuckled the pack. A dark furry face with big green eyes stared up at her. "Why, you have a cat," she said accusingly. "Don't you know they're not allowed here?"

Peter flushed. "Father said I could bring him," he said stiffly. "His name is Mouschi." He bent down to pick the cat up. But Moushi jumped out of the bag and dashed under a table.

"Anne, sit down," her mother said firmly. "We can discuss the cat later. Peter, please join us." She gestured toward an empty chair.

Anne returned to her seat, scowling. It was unfair that Peter could bring his cat, and she had to leave hers behind. On the other hand, perhaps someone else's cat was better than no cat at all!

She regarded the newcomer thoughtfully. Yes, Peter was certainly attractive, with clear blue eyes and thick wavy brown hair. But she had met him before, and he always seemed quite shy and awkward around girls. She would much rather have Hello to talk to.

Half an hour later Mr. and Mrs. van Pels came puffing up the stairs. Small, lively Auguste van Pels was clutching a hatbox—without the hat. It held a chamber pot instead. "I just don't feel at home without my chamber pot," she announced. For his part, Hermann van Pels had brought a foldable tea tray.

*People cling to the strangest things!* thought Anne, trying not to laugh.

Now that their annex family was complete, they needed a party to celebrate. Anne came up with the perfect occasion—the first anniversary of the Gies wedding on July 16. Jan and Miep were invited as guests of honor, and Mrs. Frank and Mrs. van Pels prepared a very special supper.

The night before, Anne stole down to her father's old office to use the typewriter. She wanted to type out a formal menu. That way they could pretend they were eating in an expensive French restaurant.

"Dinner, offered by The Secret Annex on the occasion of the anniversary of the marriage of Mr. and Mrs. Gies," she typed at the top of a sheet of paper. Underneath she listed the courses:

> *Bouillon a la Hunzestraat* (soup named after the street where Jan and Miep lived)
>
> *Roastbeaf Scholze* (the name of their butcher)
>
> *Salade Richelieu* (Richelieu salad)
>
> *1 Pomme de terre* (potato)
>
> *Sauce de Boeuf* (gravy)

At the bottom, she typed, "Coffee with sugar, cream, and several surprises."

That Saturday night Jan and Miep arrived

in their best clothes. The seven annex residents and their special guests crowded around the common-room table. After a delicious dinner Otto Frank rose to give a toast. "To our faithful helpers," he said, raising his glass to Jan and Miep. "May they find all the happiness they so richly deserve."

"Hear, hear," cheered Mr. van Pels, his face red.

Anne looked over at Jan and Miep, sitting close together and holding hands. So much had happened since their wedding a year ago. Then she was lighthearted and free, surrounded by dozens of friends. Now she was shut up in a small space, with only a few people for company. Then she could sit in the sun or walk along the canals. Now she couldn't even open a window. And who knew when she'd be able to go outside again!

Yet, as her father said, they were all alive

and together, and that was the most important thing.

She decided to think of the annex as a very strange hotel. And she was having an unusual adventure!

# CHAPTER EIGHT

# QUIET AS MICE

Anne was eager for news from the outside. "Have you seen my friends?" she asked Miep when she paid her daily visit. "Where is my cat, Moortje? Have you talked to Jacque or Hanneli?"

"Moortje is with your neighbors," Miep replied, "probably getting very fat and happy. But I can tell you little about your friends."

Patiently Miep explained that she couldn't go around asking people questions. It would look too suspicious. After all, everyone believed that the Franks had escaped to Switzerland. Miep could not let anyone know she was in contact with them.

Anne hung her head. It was all so confusing. What had happened to her old life? She felt as if she had put a book down in the middle of the story—and didn't know the ending! She missed her friends terribly. Margot and Peter were no substitute for Jacque or Hello. They were mopey and boring—just no fun at all.

Life in the annex was much the same, day after day. During the morning they had to be quiet as mice. On no account could the workers in the office warehouse below them hear a sound. No water could be run, no toilets flushed, no shoes worn. If they had to move, they tiptoed around in their stocking feet.

After four hours Anne was stiff and sore and ready to scream. It was hard for Mrs. Quackenbush to keep still that long!

At noon the warehouse men would go home for lunch. Then the helpers would come visit. Miep would get the day's shopping list from Mrs. Frank. Bep Voskuijl, the office secretary, would stop by to have lunch. Bep was quiet and shy, with thick glasses and a pleasant smile. Victor Kugler and Johannes Kleiman, who were running the business for Mr. Frank, would fetch newspapers and news from the outside world. Sometimes Mr. Kugler brought Anne her favorite magazine—*Cinema & Theater.*

Bep's father, Hans Voskuijl, had also been let into the secret. At Mr. Kugler's suggestion, Mr. Voskuijl built a bookcase on the outside of the annex door. It could swing open and shut and was fastened with a hook at the top. Miep filled the bookcase with old account books. No one who didn't know the secret would ever guess what lay behind those books.

Jan Gies was in charge of finding ration tickets for the annex family. During the war all Dutch people were issued coupons for different kinds of food, clothing, and other necessities. One coupon might be for bread, another for sugar, a third for butter. After the Franks disappeared, they were no longer issued their own ration cards. So Jan bought cards through the underground resistance network. Miep took the coupons with her when she went out to buy food.

After lunch there followed another four hours of quiet. Then—freedom! The workers would go home, and Miep would sneak up to let them know it was safe to come out. Everyone would troop downstairs to the big office below—and scatter.

Mr. Frank and Mr. van Pels would look through business correspondence and orders. Even though they were in hiding, they were still interested in how Opekta was doing. For exercise Peter moved crates and barrels in the warehouse. Anne and Margot practiced their dance routines. Sometimes Miep left them filing work to do.

And everyone would gather around the big

Philips radio in Mr. Frank's old office. The British broadcasting network, the BBC, was their lifeline to the outer world.

At 7:30 every night the BBC broadcast Radio Orange from London. The Dutch national anthem played, and Queen Wilhemina spoke some encouraging words. In September the radio announced that Crown Princess Juliana was expecting another baby. Anne was thrilled. Juliana was in Canada with her two daughters while her husband Prince Bernhard fought with the English. A new baby would give them all hope for the future.

One night soon after they arrived, Mr. van Pels turned the dial to the German network by mistake. The hate-filled words of Adolf Hitler filled the room.

"Please turn that off," Edith Frank said, putting her hands over her ears. "I can't bear it."

"I agree," Otto Frank said grimly. "We will

not listen to the lies of these barbarians. We must make a pledge never to turn that station on again."

"Except to hear classical music?" Margot suggested. "Surely Mozart and Beethoven cannot be considered barbarians." Everyone nodded their heads in agreement.

"And I think only civilized languages should be spoken in the annex," Anne chimed in. "Like Dutch or English. No German."

"That will be easier for some of us than for others," said Mrs. van Pels, putting down her knitting. The van Pels had also emigrated from Germany, and Mrs. van Pels did not speak Dutch or English very well. Neither did Anne's mother.

"No, I think Anne is right," said Mr. Frank. "This will give us all a chance to polish up our language skills. Right, Annelein?"

"I want to be fluent in English and French," Anne declared. "After we get out of here, I am going to be a sophisticated traveler. A citizen of the world!"

Everyone laughed. Mrs. Frank, though, looked at her daughter somberly and shook her head.

Anne was annoyed. Her mother was always so gloomy! Just because she was pessimistic about the future, didn't mean Anne had to be too.

After lights-out Anne lay in bed and listened to the sounds of the night. The squeak of her sister's bedsprings. Mr. van Pels snoring. A rat scurrying in the attic. A thousand unwanted thoughts came rushing into her head. What if they were discovered? What if the Allies didn't defeat the Germans? What was happening to their friends? Had any of them been transported to the east? Were they in concentration camps?

And then she would hear the bells of the Westertoren, the nearby clock tower, and feel better. Every fifteen minutes, all day and all night, the carillon of the famous church chimed a melody. Everyone else complained that the bells kept them awake. But Anne loved the deep, rolling sound. The Westertoren was like a "faithful friend," she wrote in her diary. Comforted, she would fall asleep.

A month later, at lunchtime, they had a real fright. Anne was reciting some poetry to her father when suddenly they heard banging outside the annex door. "Shh!" warned Otto Frank, raising a finger to his mouth. They listened intently. "It sounds like the carpenter filling the fire extinguisher," he whispered. "Nobody told us he was coming."

"I better warn Bep not to come downstairs," Anne said. "She's having lunch with the van Pels." She ran up to warn her, then crept downstairs again. Anne and her father stood near the door, waiting for the carpenter to finish. They heard him leave the landing.

And then someone started banging on the bookcase!

*Oh no!* Anne thought. *They've found us!* She was so frightened, she thought she would faint.

"Open up," a familiar voice bellowed. "It's me." It was Mr. Kleiman!"

It turned out that the carpenter had already left. When Mr. Kleiman came up to give Bep the all clear, he found that the hook on the bookcase was stuck. He was shaking it to try to get in. All was well.

Five months after they went into hiding, the radio had great news. The British and Americans had landed in North Africa! After they captured North Africa from the Germans and Italians, they would move up into Europe from the south. *Perhaps the war will be over soon,* Anne thought, *just as father says it will.*

On November 10, British prime minister Winston Churchill came on the radio to tell the world about the Allied plans. "Now this is not the end," he informed his listeners. "It is not even the beginning of the end. But it is, perhaps, the end of the beginning."

*I guess the war will not end soon after all,* Anne thought. *But it* will *end—eventually!*

# CHAPTER NINE

# DEAREST KITTY

"Eat some more spinach, Anne!" Mrs. van Pels demanded. "You'll shrivel away to nothing."

Anne looked down at the watery spinach and pale white cabbage on her plate. It was none of Mrs. van Pels's business what she ate, she told herself. She was sick and tired of being told what to do. Especially by that nosy old busybody!

But she would try to be polite. "No, thank you," she replied. "I think I'll stick to potatoes."

"The child doesn't know what's good for her," Mrs. van Pels complained. "In my day we ate what our parents put before us and were thankful for the food."

"In my day children didn't like spinach either," Edith Frank said pointedly.

Mrs. van Pels took a big bite of salami and chewed vigorously. "Children today are too spoiled, that's the problem," she said, waving her fork for emphasis. "If Anne were my daughter—"

"But she's not your daughter," Otto Frank interrupted. "And her mother and I think she's doing just fine."

Anne flashed her father a look of thanks. But inside she wanted to scream.

All day long it was Anne *this*, and Anne *that*. Anne, be quiet. Anne, stand up straight. Anne, are you sure you should be reading that book? Anne, where did you ever learn to wash dishes that way? Anne, *please* be quiet.

And it wasn't just Mrs. van Pels who criticized her. Her mother did too. Obviously she'd just never be as perfect and beautiful and sweet as Margot, Anne thought bitterly.

She felt distant from her mother, who was often sharp and irritable. She felt cut off from Margot, who was moody and withdrawn.

How she needed a friend of her own to talk to!

There was only one thing to do. She'd have to make one up.

From now on she would write her diary in letter format, as if she were writing to a real person. And who would she write to? A character named Kitty Franken, from her favorite book, *Joop ter Heul.*

"Dearest Kitty," Anne began her next diary entry. To Kitty she poured out her deepest emotions. She wrote about growing up and the changes that were happening in her body. She felt restless, defiant, and needy, all at once.

With a clear eye she described the other inhabitants of the Secret Annex. Mr. van Pels, she wrote, could be loud and greedy. He told really bad jokes, and he always took the choicest bits of food. Mrs. van Pels was silly and not very bright. Yet, Anne had to admit, she kept the common room in spick-and-span order. She and her husband were always arguing about the stupidest things—even about how to peel potatoes!

Their son Peter wasn't much better. He seemed obsessed with his health. Once he worked himself up into a tizzy because his tongue looked blue instead of pink.

Then there was her mother. She and her mother hadn't been getting along at all recently. One moment Edith treated Anne as if she were still a baby—and sometimes she wanted her to act grown up! Why couldn't she just accept Anne the way she was?

She wrote about the amusing things that happened in the annex too. For instance, there was the time that Peter tried to carry three hundred pounds of beans up to the storage area in the attic. Huffing and puffing, he lugged five sacks up the steep stairs. And then, as he almost had the sixth one up to the top—it burst! A hailstorm of beans rained down on the floor below. Anne found herself standing in an ocean of brown, while Peter roared with laughter. For months, every time she climbed the stairs, she picked up a few more beans.

Whenever Anne felt that she just couldn't bear her life one more minute, she ran to her diary. Kitty, at least, was always willing to listen. And when she wrote down all her troubles, she felt better!

Gradually she began to feel that she was a real writer, just as she had always wanted to be.

The news from outside kept getting worse. While the seven of them were safe in their cozy annex, Jews in the rest of Amsterdam were being rounded up daily. To escape, thousands of frantic people became *onderduikers* and slipped quietly into hiding.

Otto Frank called their annex family

together for a conference. "Do you think we have room for one more?" he asked them. "Where seven can live, eight can live as well."

Yes, they decided, they could squeeze one more desperate friend in. His name was Fritz Pfeffer, Miep's dentist and an old acquaintance of the Franks.

Mr. Pfeffer would move into Anne's room, and Margot would sleep next door with their parents. Anne didn't mind. She was willing to make any sacrifice to save another human being from the Nazis.

On November 16, Miep came up the stairs with their new guest. Everyone was gathered around the dining table, ready to welcome him.

"Ladies and gentlemen," Miep said, "may I present Mr. Fritz Pfeffer." She gestured to a distinguished-looking man with gray hair. "Mr. Pfeffer, I am sure you remember the Franks and the van Pelses."

Bewildered, Mr. Pfeffer looked from face to face. "But how can you be here?" he burst out. "I thought you escaped to Switzerland!" He collapsed in a chair, struck dumb with astonishment.

"That was just a story we spread to fool the secret police," Mr. Frank said. Everyone began to talk at once, explaining what had happened.

"My, my," Mr. Pfeffer repeated. He couldn't seem to get over his surprise. "And you've been here all this time." He gazed around the comfortable room. On the coal stove a pot of pea soup slowly simmered, filling the air with a delicious smell. Mouschi was curled up on a rug nearby, warm as toast. Looking at the room through Mr. Pfeffer's eyes, Anne could see how inviting it was. *We're very lucky,* she thought to herself.

Margot ladled out the soup, and Anne passed it around, trying not to spill any. As they ate, they filled Mr. Pfeffer in on everything that had happened in the four months they had been in hiding.

"I believe the young people would like to explain the rules and regulations of the annex to you," Mr. Frank said, turning to Peter.

"*Hrrmf.*" Peter cleared his throat. The tips of his ears turned red. "On behalf of the welcoming committee, I would like to present you with our official 'Guide to the Secret Annex.'" He passed Mr. Pfeffer a sheet of typed paper that had been folded to look like a brochure.

Mr. Pfeffer took out his reading glasses and ran his eyes down the paper. "The annex offers comfortable accommodations right in the heart of Amsterdam," he began, chuckling. "Furnished rooms provided free. Rest hours required from eight thirty to twelve thirty P.M. and from one thirty to five thirty P.M. from Monday to Friday. Special features include running water, private radio, and tutoring in English, French, math, and history."

105

"No German!" Anne put in.

"No German," Mr. Pfeffer agreed. He put his reading glasses on the table. "For myself, I will study Spanish. I think I may depart for South America after the war. Europe has become unbearable."

Finally Anne could not contain herself. "What is happening on the outside?" she asked. "Please tell us about our friends."

Mr. Pfeffer shook his head. "Everything is very bad," he told them grimly.

The roundups, or *razias*, of Jews had been stepped up. Everyone lived in fear of the knock on the door, the heavy boots on the stairs. Day and night people were dragged from their homes with no warning and thrown into trucks. First they were sent to the Dutch prison camp in Westerbork. From there they were transported by railway to concentration camps far away in the east.

Dreadful reports had reached Holland of

conditions in the camps. It was said that inmates were beaten, starved, humiliated. Many were killed outright.

"The BBC says that Jews are being gassed," Anne said in a low voice. "What can that mean?"

No one answered her. No one really knew.

Anne couldn't get to sleep that night. It was terrible to know that while she was snug in bed, people she knew were being murdered. And it wasn't because they had done anything wrong. It was just because they happened to be Jewish.

Hanukkah, the festival of lights, arrived on December 4 that year. The annex family held a quiet celebration around Mr. van Pels's hand-made wooden menorah. At nightfall Edith Frank lit the first candle.

Mr. Pfeffer recited the blessings in Hebrew. "You abound in blessings, Source of All, our

God, Ruler of the Universe, who performed miracles for our ancestors in those days."

The flickering candle enveloped the little group in a warm glow. *The annex is just like this little circle of light,* Anne thought. Inside there was warmth and comfort. Outside, the shadows gathered.

The next night, December 5, was the Dutch holiday Saint Nicholas Day. Every year Anne used to see Saint Nicholas, with his long white beard and red bishop's hat, riding his white horse through the streets of Amsterdam. His assistant, Black Peter, walked beside him with a sackful of presents. If children were good, they found a little gift in their shoe on holiday morn. If they were bad, Black Peter might leave them a piece of coal!

Anne had always been curious about Saint Nicholas Day. But they had never celebrated it at home, even though it was more a family than a religious holiday.

All during lunch that day, Otto Frank whispered with Miep and Bep. Anne knew something was up. After dinner he stood up and announced, "I believe our friends have prepared a treat for us. Now, if you will all follow me . . ."

Down the steep stairs to the dark alcove trooped the annex family. Mr. Frank flipped on the light, threw open the doors of the big cabinet, and cried, "Surprise!"

Anne gasped in delight. In the corner of the cabinet sat a big basket decorated with brightly colored red and green paper. A mask of Black Peter peeked over the top. "It's a Saint Nicholas basket!" she exclaimed.

She and Peter both grabbed the handle and carried the basket back up to the common room. Then Anne passed out the little wrapped presents inside. "This one's for you, Mother," she said, handing her a flat package, "and here's yours, Mrs. van Pels."

Eagerly Mrs. van Pels tore open the paper. "Why, it's a little poem," she exclaimed. "Listen to this." She read them a funny verse about how crazy she was about knitting. "And here's an embroidered needle case to go with it."

Their friends had written a poem and made a gift for each of them. Mr. Frank received a pair of handsome carved bookends. Mr. Pfeffer was delighted with his wooden picture frame. And Anne loved her Kewpie doll with the big skirt made to hold odds and ends.

"Miep and Bep must have worked on these gifts for weeks!" Anne exclaimed. "They are so kind to us."

Kindness would not make the war go away, she realized, or cause rescue to come any sooner. But it helped to know there were such good people in the world.

# CHAPTER TEN
# ECHOES OF WAR

*Ka-boom!* The German guns thundered, shaking the walls of the old house. Air-raid sirens wailed through the night.

Anne threw off her covers, grabbed her pillow, and raced into her parents' room. "Pim," she cried, throwing herself onto her father's bed. "I can't bear it. Make it stop. Please." She burst into tears and buried her head in his chest. Margot, in her folding bed across the room, put a pillow over her head.

In the spring and summer of 1943, it seemed as if the bombing would never stop. Night after night British and American planes flew over Holland and western Germany, raining bombs down on factories, airports, and military camps. From the ground German antiaircraft guns shot back, trying to strike the bombers down.

Dutch people hurried into air-raid shelters when the sirens sounded. But the people in the annex had nowhere to go. Anne wanted to run, to hide, to scream. But all she could do was cover her ears and wait until morning.

Toward dawn an especially loud burst of machine-gun fire split the air. It was followed a few seconds later by a huge explosion. A shaken Peter appeared at the Franks' door. "Come see," he said, his voice unsteady. "I think a plane has crashed."

Curiosity overcame Anne's fear. She followed Peter and her father up the ladder to the attic. Mouschi greeted them with a loud purr. He was sleeping there to guard their food supplies against rats. She scooped him up in her arms and peered out the open window. To the west a red glow filled the sky. The fires were so close by that Anne could smell the smoke.

"Don't worry," said Otto Frank, reading her thoughts. "The flames will not reach the Prinsengracht. Fire brigades will put the fire out before it gets very far."

In the dim morning light she could see a fighter plane appear overhead, traveling westward. Suddenly another big gray plane swooped out of the clouds and headed right toward it. "A German Messerschmitt!" Peter breathed.

The Allied plane circled and dived, trying to avoid the enemy's guns. But the Messerschmitt kept right on its tail. *Rat-a-tat-tat!* its machine guns rumbled. Anne gripped the window ledge, spellbound. Fire shot out of the German gun barrels—and the wing of the Allied plane exploded in a burst of orange. It had been hit!

"Jump now!" Anne begged the distant airmen. Was it her imagination, or did she see tiny dark shapes falling away from the injured aircraft? Head over tail the plane tumbled, now a blazing ball of fire. With a *boom!* it crashed in the distance.

The next evening Miep told them what had happened to the Allied airmen. Her milkman, who lived in a suburb, met four Canadians who had parachuted out of the burning plane. One of them had asked him for a light for his cigarette. A short time later, they were arrested by the German security police.

Usually there was a lull in the bombing during daylight hours. Anne, Margot, and Peter, the three students, spent their time hunched over their books. They longed to go back to school when the war was over, and they didn't want to be left behind.

Anne had a strict schedule, planned by Otto Frank. On a typical morning she might translate some Dutch history into English, read eighteenth-century European history, and study Brazilian geography. In the afternoon she might tackle a biography of Charles V of Prussia, read an English novel, take a French test—and learn about the monkeys of South America.

And then—there was algebra! She absolutely detested math. Sometimes she grumbled and refused to do her algebra lesson for the day. But her father would put his foot down. "I'll take away your diary," he warned her.

Oh, no, anything but that!

Most of the time she was grateful she loved to read so much. Sometimes she looked around her parents' bedroom in the middle of the day, when they all had to be quiet. Her father, seated on the saggy bed, was reading the English writer Charles Dickens. Her mother was deep into a contemporary novel. Margot, her glasses slipping down her nose, was buried in a biography of composer Franz Liszt.

What, oh what, would they have done if they didn't have books?

Anne's special passion was Greek mythology. She loved the colorful tales of gods and heroes. Sometimes she got the stories mixed up, though. There were so many heroes, and so many monsters! Was it Perseus or Theseus who had slain the half man–half bull minotaur? Was it Theseus or Perseus who rescued Andromeda from the sea serpent? And what were the seven labors of Hercules, anyway?

When Anne wasn't reading, she was writing. Her father had forbidden anyone to look at her diary. That way, she could write about anything she wanted. Kitty would understand, she knew. Kitty wouldn't think she was being rude, or talking back, or complaining too much. If she didn't tell someone her deepest thoughts, she'd burst!

She wrote about all the funny and frightening things that happened in the annex:

The day Peter put his hand down on the attic floor—and was bitten by a rat.

116

The time Mouschi got fleas—and everybody started itching.

The night burglars got into the safe in the downstairs office—and stole all their sugar coupons.

The week Mr. Pfeffer got his dentist's drill—and practiced on each of them in turn!

Mr. Pfeffer, her roommate, turned out to be really annoying. Not only did he snore all night, but he hogged their bedroom during the day. All morning he hunched over the little desk in their room. In the afternoon, when he wasn't taking a nap, he sat there too.

It really wasn't fair, Anne decided. She also needed her privacy once in a while. She screwed up her courage and decided to confront him.

"Mr. Pfeffer," she said, as politely as possible, "I have a favor to ask. Might I use our table two afternoons a week, from four o'clock to five thirty? I have a lot of work to do and I need to concentrate undisturbed."

Mr. Pfeffer looked startled. "What kind of work do you have, child?" he asked. "Mythology and writing stories? Bah! This is not work." He became quite red in the face. "I have real studying to do, not some adolescent nonsense. No, you cannot have the desk."

Anne could feel her anger rising. "My French and English are every bit as important as your Spanish," she retorted. "I have to study to keep up with my grade in school."

"Ah, so now if someday you fail your exams, you will blame me," Mr. Pfeffer grumbled. He banged his fist on the desk. "I have never seen such a selfish child. You insist on getting your own way about everything! In my day, children were seen and not heard. Your parents should have taught you that."

Seething, Anne spun on her heels and walked away. There was no use talking to such a man! That evening she told her father what had happened. He smoothed things over with

Mr. Pfeffer. From then on, the desk was hers two afternoons a week.

Nineteen-forty-three crept slowly on. In the evening they would cluster around the radio and listen to the news. They kept close track of the progress of the war. The Russians beat the Germans at Stalingrad in January 1943. The British and Americans took North Africa in May. By September they had landed in Italy and were battling the Germans there.

Help was coming—but very slowly. Why didn't the Allies surge over the English Channel to Holland and save them?

"Any day now," the optimistic Otto Frank would repeat. "The invasion will come any day!"

And always there were the dreadful rumors about what was happening to the Jews.

One night Anne had a dream. Her old friend Hanneli appeared before her, dressed in rags. Her hair was matted, her face dirty.

Behind her loomed a vast, dark wasteland. "Oh, Anne, where are you?" she cried. "I am lost and cannot find my way home. Please, come rescue me. Anne, I need you!"

With a start, Anne awoke, terrified. She knew what the dream meant. Hanneli had been captured by the Nazis and sent to a concentration camp while she, Anne, was safe in the annex. Anne felt guilty and helpless, but there was nothing she could do.

*Dear God,* she prayed. *Keep Hanneli and her family well, and bring them back to us. Bring back Sanne, and Jacque, and Hello, and Ilse. Perform a miracle, as you did for the Israelites so long ago, and keep us safe.*

The Friday before New Year's Day 1944, all of the helpers trooped upstairs for a small celebration. Jan had scrounged some black-market beer for the grown-ups. Edith Frank brewed some fake coffee for the young people.

As everyone watched, Miep whipped the tea

towel off her surprise. It was a golden brown spice cake, Anne's favorite.

"You used your precious ration of eggs and butter to bake us a cake," Anne cried, giving Miep a kiss.

Then she noticed the words carved into the top of the cake. They gave her an idea. "I'd like to propose a toast," Anne said, holding up her coffee cup. Around the table everyone raised their glasses.

"Peace 1944," Anne declared.

# CHAPTER ELEVEN
# A SPECIAL FRIENDSHIP

"Five inches," Otto Frank said, marking a line on the wall behind Anne's head. He was keeping a record of Anne's height on a growth chart in his room. "That's how much you've grown in the year and a half we've been in hiding, Annelein."

"No wonder nothing fits anymore!" she exclaimed. "Look at my sweater. The sleeves are halfway up my arm!" She turned around and held out her scrawny wrists to Miep, who had just come in the door. She looked so comical that Miep started to laugh.

"You may snicker," Anne said in mock anger. "But imagine me, back at school, in these clothes! What would the teachers say?"

She pretended to be walking down the school corridor. "Oh, hello, Mr. K. What, you think my clothes are, shall we say, a bit too daring? Why, they're straight off the Paris runway!"

She posed like a fashion model. "For spring 1944, the latest in peekaboo blouses! Don't even try to button it up. It's supposed to be too small. Just enjoy the natural air-conditioning." She gestured to her skirt, which came up above her knee. "Short skirts are all the rage this year. Try to ignore the stares you get when you walk down the street.

"As for shoes?" She sat down on a chair and tried to tug on her old shoes, now two sizes too small. Dramatically she threw them into a corner of the room. "Ahh, who needs shoes when you can experience the bliss of bare feet?" she said, wiggling her toes in the air.

"Bravo!" cried Miep, clapping her hands. "However, I think I have a solution for your little shoe problem." She set her shopping bag down on a table—and took out a pair of dark red high heels! "These are for you!"

"Oh, Miep, they're so beautiful," Anne squealed. Hurriedly she put them on, then tried to walk. "Of course, it will take me a while before I get used to them," she said, giggling.

She went out into the hall, wobbling just a bit. Peter van Pels was just coming in from the main office with the evening's bread. "Look, Peter," she said, twirling around on her toes. "Aren't they simply divine?"

Peter gazed at her for a long moment. "Y-yes," he said, blushing. "They're quite flattering. You look very nice, Anne." He gave her a quick smile, then ran up the stairs to the common room.

Anne gazed after him, lost in thought. Lately she had caught Peter staring at her when he thought she wasn't looking. What was he thinking? she wondered. He was so quiet, it was hard to tell. But he did seem to be thinking about her!

Her father followed her out into the hall. "You are becoming a little woman," he said, giving her a kiss on her forehead. "Before you know it, you will be all grown up!"

*Not yet,* Anne thought. *Right now, all I want to be is a teenager—and have some fun!*

That winter, when Anne was fourteen-and-a-half, she could feel herself changing day by day. Every morning she studied herself in the mirror. Was her nose a little slimmer? Her mouth a little wider? Certainly her hair had grown long and luxuriant. Even though it was difficult to obtain shampoo, she kept it clean. Every day she would put on her beige, flowered combing shawl and brush her curls out until they were smooth and silky. Every night she set her hair in pin curls. She loved trying out new hairstyles. What actress did she want to look like today?

Mostly, though, it was the changes inside

her that she noticed. Sometimes she felt as light and carefree as a bird. She wanted to beat her wings and fly out the window into the big wide world.

Other times she felt as though her heart would break. One moment she would be peeling potatoes or washing the dishes. The next she was blinking back tears. Off she would rush to the bathroom, the only place she could be alone. After ten minutes of sobbing, she would dry her tears and return to the common room.

There was no use falling apart in front of her family, she knew. They had to be strong for one another.

She just wished she had someone to talk to, someone her own age. She loved Margot, but they were too different. Her sister kept all her emotions bottled up. Anne let hers all out. She wanted to talk to someone who was willing to talk back!

Maybe that someone could be Peter. Every time she noticed his warm blue eyes looking at her, she felt pleased and excited. *Maybe he really wants to be friends,* she thought, *but is just too bashful.*

One Sunday morning she was up in the attic looking through a box of books when Peter came up the ladder. "I was looking for you," he began. "Mr. Pfeffer wants you to come down and wash out the tub. He says you left it dirty, and he wants to take a bath."

"What an old fusspot," she said, sighing. "Why didn't you tell him to do it himself?"

Peter hung his head. "If I tried to tell him what I really thought, I would just start tripping over my words," he explained. "I get tongue-tied when I'm angry. That's why I admire you, Anne. You always know exactly what to say."

"Me?" Anne said, laughing. "My problem is that I don't know when to shut up. You know, they used to call me Mrs. Quackenbush at school. And I must say I deserved it."

"Well, that's better than being too shy to say anything."

Peter sat down on a crate and they had a long talk about school and parents. Anne had completely lost track of time when an annoyed Mr. Pfeffer stuck his head through the trapdoor. "Anne, I must insist," he said.

"Coming, Mr. Pfeffer," Anne replied. As she got up to leave, Peter winked at her.

Now Anne had something to look forward to every day—seeing Peter. She might run into him on the staircase, or at lunch, or around the radio in the evening—and her heart would jump. She wasn't actually falling in love with him, she told herself. But she longed for a very special friendship. Did he feel that way about her, too?

One day she read him parts of "Eva's Dream," a fairy tale she was working on. It was about a little girl who dreams she is walking in a beautiful garden. There she meets an elf who introduces her to all the flowers. She meets the spoiled rose, the selfish chestnut tree, and the kind bluebell.

People, too, can be spoiled, selfish, or kind, the elf tells her. Eva can choose what kind of girl she wants to be.

"And when Eva wakes up," Anne concluded, "she is known as the kindest, most helpful girl for miles around."

She turned to Peter. "I want to be like Eva," she said. "But it's so hard!"

Early one morning she went up to the attic to get a deep breath of fresh air before the day started. Peter was already there, looking out the window. Anne went over and stood beside him. Over the rooftops of Amsterdam, seagulls glided through the clear blue sky. The bare chestnut tree in the courtyard shone in the sun, ready for spring. In its topmost branches a small gray nest waited for a new family to arrive. Nature seemed fresh and young and new, and everything was beginning again.

Anne pressed close to Peter, her hand almost touching his. "On a day like this," she said softly, "aren't you just glad to be alive?"

# CHAPTER 12
# BECOMING A WRITER

"Anne, come listen!" Margot Frank called. She poked her head into Mr. Kleiman's office, where Anne was finishing up some filing for Bep. "There's something on the radio you should hear."

It was the evening of March 28, 1944, and the annex family was downstairs doing chores and relaxing. Anne stuck the last folder back in the file cabinet and followed Margot into the big comfortable private office. The others were listening to Radio Orange, broadcast from London by the Dutch government in exile.

"Gerrit Bolkestein is speaking," Otto Frank told Anne in a whisper. "He's the minister of education and culture."

Anne leaned close to the radio to catch every word. "We owe it to future generations to provide a complete historical record of this time of trial," Bolkestein was saying. "Everyone in Holland should save their diaries and letters from these years."

"He's talking about you," Mrs. van Pels said, nudging Anne.

"Yes," Anne said. She was straining to hear. "Hush, please."

"We will collect them after the war," the minister continued. "Only simple writings from ordinary citizens will provide a full record of the nobility and suffering of the Dutch people."

The stately chords of the Dutch national anthem closed out the broadcast. Then everybody started talking at once.

"You could be a published writer," Margot pointed out.

"Maybe I could turn my diary into a novel,"

Anne mused. "I could call it . . . *Het Acterhuis*. The Secret Annex."

Peter looked excited. "That sounds like a spy novel. A real best-seller."

"Then we would finally discover what you've been writing all this time," Mrs. van Pels said in a teasing voice.

Anne grinned, but her thoughts were far away. Yes, she longed to be published! She had even asked Mr. Kleiman about submitting her fairy tales to a magazine. But he thought it was too risky.

Now, though, she had a goal to work toward. Eagerly she went back to her earliest diary entries and started rereading them. Her thirteenth birthday seemed so long ago! Then, all she had cared about was school, and clothes, and being popular. There was almost nothing in her diary about her family or the German occupation of Holland. She had not even written about being Jewish and having to wear a yellow star.

Clearly she would have to fill her future readers in on everything she had seen and experienced for the last two years. What was it really like to be a Jewish teenager in Europe during the Nazi occupation?

Beginning with her earliest entries, she began to rewrite her whole diary. She didn't have any new notebooks, because paper was so scarce. Instead Miep and Bep gave her thin blue and pink sheets of tracing paper from the office. Writing in long straight lines with no cross-outs, she filled each sheet, front and back. Carefully she placed the sheets in the leather briefcase her father gave her. No one, he promised her, would dare peek inside.

She also didn't want to embarrass anybody by using real names in her published book. No, she would make up pseudonyms. She wrote out a list of possibilities:

*Johannes Kleiman—Mr. Koophius*
*Victor Kugler—Mr. Kraler*

*Miep Gies—Miep van Santen*
*Jan Gies—Henk van Santen*
*Bep Voskuijl—Elli Vossen*
*The van Pels family—the van Daan family*
*Fritz Pfeffer—Albert Dussel*

Perhaps, she thought, she should also change the name of her own family. The Franks could become the Robinses . . .

Every day she sped though page after page, rewriting the old and writing the new. Now she had a purpose, a way to be useful. She didn't want an ordinary life like most women, who cooked and cleaned and raised a family and were forgotten. No, she wanted her name to live on, like that of Charles Dickens, or William Shakespeare, or the German writer Johann Wolfgang von Goethe. She too would be a writer—the writer Anne Frank.

And even if she weren't really famous, she

thought, at least she would have brought happiness to others.

Her imagination was on fire, and she wrote on.

The evening of Sunday, April 9, most of the annex went to the common room to listen to a special radio show. The German station was playing music by the Austrian composer Wolfgang Amadeus Mozart. Curled up in an easy chair with her sewing, Anne listened to *Eine Kleine Nachtmusik*—"A Little Night Music." It was one of her favorite pieces. The sweet music stirred her very soul.

Every time she despaired about the human race, she remembered Mozart. Surely such divine music proved that people were really good at heart!

The first notes of a violin sonata had just sounded when Peter burst into the room. "Uh, Mr. Frank," he stuttered, "Could you come look at my English lesson? I'm having trouble with a translation."

Not only Otto Frank but also Mr. Pfeffer and Mr. van Pels got up and quickly left the room. Mrs. van Pels put down her knitting and looked wide-eyed at the remaining women. Her hand rose to her mouth. "It's not really a translation," she said, her voice trembling. "There's something wrong, I can tell."

"Perhaps we had better turn off the radio," Edith Frank suggested.

The four women sat in silence, straining to hear. Five minutes crept by, then ten. A loud *crash!* echoed through the house. Anne felt the blood drain from her face. Her hands felt cold and clammy. *Please, don't let me faint*, she thought.

The suspense was unbearable.

Finally Mr. Frank stuck his head through the door. "Lights out," he ordered curtly. "There's been a burglary." Then he disappeared again. Mrs. van Pels switched off the lamp, and the room was plunged into darkness.

Anne knew that burglaries were common throughout Holland. Desperate people looking for food—or goods that could be sold to get food—were breaking into houses and offices. Robbers were attracted by the barrels of spices stored in the downstairs warehouse. It didn't matter so much if supplies were stolen. But what if the thieves heard noises upstairs and suspected there were people in hiding? And then, even worse, what if they told the police?

There was a commotion on the stairs and all four men burst into the common room. "The police are coming!" Otto Frank said urgently. "Everyone must be quiet!"

Peter plopped down on the floor next to Anne. He was breathing hard, as if he'd been running. "Tell me what happened," she whispered.

"I was downstairs when I noticed that a

panel had been taken out of the warehouse door," Peter explained. "I rushed back up to warn everyone else and by the time we came down again, we could hear the burglars!"

"I think you were awfully brave," Anne asked. "Why didn't you hide?"

"Because Father yelled out 'Police!' hoping to scare them off," Peter explained. "They dropped whatever they were taking and ran away. Then we began to nail the panel back on the door. But suddenly a flashlight shone through the door!"

"The burglars?"

"No, just a man and a woman passing by on the street, I think. That's when we took off and locked the door. Now we're afraid—"

"Shh!" a voice said urgently.

"We're afraid they'll notify the police!" Peter ended.

An hour later they could hear footsteps in the office below. The eight fugitives froze, trying not to move a muscle. The footsteps came closer, plodding through the front office, then down the hallway and up the stairs. The policeman—if that's who it was—rattled the bookcase, shone the flashlight about, then shook the bookcase again.

The footsteps moved away.

But they might be back.

That night was the longest Anne had ever known. No one dared make any noise for fear the police had left a guard in the office. So they lay down on the floor and tried to rest. Even though Mrs. van Pels lent Anne a blanket and pillow, she could not sleep. She was shivering too hard.

The next morning when Miep and Jan arrived, Anne threw herself into Miep's arms. "We were so scared," she cried.

Looking grim, Jan explained what had happened. "The night watchman on the Prinsengracht noticed the break-in and called the police," he said. "He and the policeman were the ones who searched the building. You were very lucky this time. No one saw you. But from now on, you must stay upstairs. Never go down. Especially when you hear a noise!"

Never go downstairs again! The noose was growing tighter, Anne thought. The moment they forgot that they were in hiding, they were brought back to reality.

Luckily she still had her beloved attic. That evening she and Peter stole upstairs and sat next to each other on a dusty crate. He put his arm around her, and she leaned her head on his shoulder. They stayed there for a long time, gazing outside as the darkness crept over the city.

Anne didn't want the spell to end. But her father was waiting for her to say their nightly bedside prayers. "I've got to go," she whispered, and slipped out from under Peter's arm.

"Wait a moment," he said. Then he leaned over and gave her a little peck, half on her lips and half on her cheek.

It was her first kiss.

# CHAPTER THIRTEEN
# HOPE AND FEAR

In May 1944, all of Europe held its breath, waiting for the Allied invasion.

Yet still the invasion didn't come. Otto Frank had a bet with Auguste van Pels that the British and Americans would cross the English Channel by May 20. When the date came and went, she demanded her payment. "Five jars of yogurt, Otto," she said, holding her hand out.

Food had become the most precious commodity of all. Many days all they had to eat was cereal, bread, and potatoes. Vegetables—boiled lettuce and spinach—were available twice a week. Eggs, butter, yogurt, and liverwurst were saved for special occasions. The adults groused endlessly about the food. Anne didn't mind it so much really. At least they were safe.

It was all a big adventure, she told herself. Her life was like a Hollywood movie. It had good guys—the brave Jews in hiding, courageous Dutch helpers, and stout resistance fighters. And it had bad guys—the brutal German secret police and their traitorous Dutch allies. The plot had moments of suspense, when the fugitives were almost discovered by the Nazis. And it had romance, when the young heroine fell in love with the brave young man. Well, not really fell in love, she corrected herself. Maybe fell in *like* would be more accurate!

Anne herself, of course, was the heroine. And she was waiting to be rescued—by British and American knights in shining armored tanks!

Hiding for two years had brought her fear and hardship. But she liked to think that she had also gained wisdom.

Sometimes she thought about war, and how

horrible and senseless it was, and why countries would fight each other in the first place. It couldn't just be that some officers and politicians were evil and greedy. No, ordinary people must also have an inner demon that made them want to hate, and destroy, and kill. If they didn't, the leaders would have no one to follow them. War, she decided, would not end until people were transformed from the inside out.

Sometimes she saw the world as one vast wasteland. Outside the annex were forces waiting to destroy them. Then she would remember Mozart, and Miep, and her father. People could be good, and pure, and selfless, she knew. They were capable of creating works of great beauty. Perhaps all would be well in the end, and they would know peace once more.

Anyhow, writers needed lots of different experiences to write about. She had to have an interesting life—so she could write an exciting book!

* * * *

"Wake up, Margot, it's happened!" Anne screamed, shaking her sister out of bed. "The news just came over the BBC! The invasion has started!"

It was 7:30 in the morning on June 6, 1944. A huge force of Allied troops had landed on the coast of France and launched a major assault on German shoreline defenses. Inch by inch, soldiers fought their way up the beaches. Further inland, paratroopers jumped behind enemy lines to take control of roads and bridges.

All morning the annex family hovered around the radio on the kitchen table. Everyone was tense with excitement. "This is D-day," the BBC announced in German, Dutch, French, and English. "The Day of Days."

Mr. Frank tacked a map of the coast of France up on the wall. "This way we'll be able to track the progress of the Allied forces," he said. "Look, I have red pins for the Allies. Let's put the first pin here, at Asnelles."

"And another at Isigny and one at Sainte-Mère-Église," Anne chimed in excitedly. "And maybe one behind the German lines, where the paratroopers are landing."

"How long do you think it will take the army to get to Amsterdam?" Mr. van Pels asked, peering at the map.

"Oh, two, three, maybe six months at the most," Otto Frank guessed.

"Maybe we'll be back in school by fall," Margot exclaimed. She took both of Anne's hands in hers and began to swing her around. "Oh, Anne, just think."

"Freedom!" Anne sang, spinning faster and faster. It was wonderful to see her usually subdued sister so exuberant. Giggling, the two girls collapsed on the floor.

At lunchtime Jan Gies appeared with a big smile on his face. "Cocoa!" he exclaimed, waving a packet in the air. "I've been saving it for an extra-special occasion."

"General Eisenhower will be speaking at twelve," Miep announced, appearing behind her husband. "We thought we could all listen together."

A few minutes later they were each holding a cup of hot cocoa, and Peter turned up the volume on the radio. The voice of American general Dwight D. Eisenhower, supreme commander of the Allied troops, filled the room. He seemed to be speaking personally to the Secret Annex.

"People of Western Europe!" he said in his flat American accent. "A landing was made this morning on the coast of France by troops of the Allied Expeditionary Force. This landing is part of the concerted United Nations plan for the liberation of Europe. I have this message for all of you . . . the hour of your liberation is approaching."

"Liberation," Edith Frank murmured, tears welling in her eyes. "We will be freed. Can it be true?"

General Eisenhower continued. "All patriots, men and women, young and old, have a part to play in the achievement of final victory."

"To victory!" Otto Frank declared, clinking his cocoa cup with Anne's.

"To victory!" echoed the others, raising their cups in a toast.

*Friends are on the way,* Anne thought.

Anne's fifteenth birthday was celebrated only six days later. Everyone arrived with a present: She got candies from Miep, notebooks from Bep, art history books from her parents, yogurt, jam, cookies—and, wonder of wonders, actual fresh cream cheese from Mr. Kugler.

Her most touching gift, though, came from Peter. He took her aside before the party and thrust a lovely bunch of lavender peonies into her hand. "Happy birthday," he said, his cheeks pink.

She reached up and kissed him softly. Peter was so sweet, she thought. True, he had never become the confidante she had longed for. He was not as interested in books and ideas as she was. Yet he was a genuinely kind and thoughtful person. She was lucky to have found a friend like him in hiding.

Weeks later, on a beautiful July evening, she, Peter, and Margot went up to the attic to breathe in the soft summer air. All day long they had been in the common room making strawberry jam. A friend of Miep's had presented her with crates and crates of fresh strawberries, straight from the country. Miep had locked the front door, and the whole annex had pitched in, hulling, washing, and boiling. For every strawberry Anne had cleaned, she had popped one in her mouth. Now she felt full and content.

"This is the life," Peter said lazily. He was stretched out on the floor, petting his cat. "When all this is over, I'm going to go someplace warm, maybe to the Dutch West Indies to work on a rubber plantation. I never want to be cold or hungry again."

"I want to help people, the way we've been helped," Margot said softly. "After the war there will be so many Jewish orphans. If I'm a nurse in Palestine, I can look after the children."

"I'm sure you'll be a wonderful nurse; you're so gentle and caring," Anne told her. She stood up and stared out at the silver moon, shining above the rooftops. "I don't know if I can ever settle down in one place, though. I'm going to travel, to Paris, and London, and America, meet fascinating people and do exciting things."

"And then you're going to be a famous writer," Peter prompted her.

"Yes," said Anne with a twinkle in her eye.

"I am going to be a famous writer. Just wait and see!"

The Allied army kept advancing. By early August they were racing toward Paris. A group of high-ranking German officers, realizing they were losing the war, tried to assassinate Hitler. The attempt failed, but, Anne hoped, perhaps the next one would succeed. The Secret Annex waited. Surely it could not be long now.

The morning of August 4 dawned clear and sunny. Upstairs at 263 Prinsengracht, the annex family prepared for another day much like the ones they had known for the past two years and one month. Downstairs, the office staff arrived for work. The sound of ringing phones and clattering typewriters filled the building.

Anne was busy studying when the warehouse door opened at 10:30 that morning and a man in the uniform of the German secret police strode in. She did not hear the heavy boots on the stairs, the German voices barking out orders. She did not hear the SS man command Mr. Kugler to take him to the Jews in hiding.

But she did hear the rattle at the bookcase and the bang it made when it was flung open. Victor Kugler came into her parent's room, his face white. "Gestapo," he whispered.

The SS officer shoved past him, a pistol in his hand. "Hands up!" he ordered Edith Frank and her daughters. Anne stood up, dropping her book on the desk. Wordlessly all three raised their hands in the air.

Anne was numb, unable to think or feel. It was as if she were watching the scene through the wrong end of a telescope, a long distance away.

"Here are the others," a voice called out. Anne's father, Mr. and Mrs. van Pels, and Peter stumbled down the stairs, followed by two Dutch policemen.

"Where are your valuables?" the SS officer barked at Otto Frank. "Show me your money." Mr. Frank motioned toward the wooden chest he kept in a closet.

The policemen started to ransack the room, opening closets and drawers and throwing their contents onto the floor. The SS officer spied the leather briefcase in a corner. "What is this, then?" he asked. He turned it upside down. Out flew hundreds of sheets of blue and pink paper, some notebooks, and a small red and beige diary.

In her trance, Anne did not even look at them.

"All right then, everyone get what they need," the SS man said. "We're leaving." Anne and the others scrambled to find the bags they had packed long before, in case of an emergency.

Five minutes later the eight annex residents trudged down the steep office stairs for the last time. They had been betrayed.

# CHAPTER FOURTEEN

# NIGHT FALLS

A leaden gray sky hung heavily over Bergen-Belsen concentration camp in Germany. It was early February 1945, and a light snow had fallen the day before. From watchtowers high above the camp, German guards looked down on hundreds of makeshift wooden barracks. There tens of thousands of people huddled together, clinging to survival. Illness, hunger, and the cold claimed nearly a thousand lives a day. Anyone who tried to escape—or who even approached the barbed-wire fence— would be shot.

Anne had already been in this camp four months. Now Margot, with whom she shared a bunk, was desperately ill with typhus, a deadly disease carried by lice. This evening she was hand-feeding her a bowl of thin soup. "Take just a few sips," she urged, holding the bowl to her sister's feverish lips.

"Anne!" a hoarse voice called out urgently. Anne looked up to see a thin figure coming toward her through the crowded barracks. It was Auguste van Pels. But no one who had seen her in the Secret Annex would have recognized her now. Like Anne, she had short-cropped hair and wore the zebra-striped pajamas of the concentration camp.

"I have the most amazing news," Mrs. van Pels told her. "I talked to your old friend Hanneli Goslar on the other side of the fence. She is here, in Bergen-Belsen. She's waiting for you."

Hanneli! Anne felt a sudden surge of hope. She'd thought Hanneli must have perished in the camps a long time ago. "Here," she said, hastily handing the soup bowl to Mrs. van Pels. "See if you can get her to eat."

Anne hurried out into the frigid night, zigzagging to avoid the searchlight beams that swept over the ground. When she reached the barbed wire, she softly called out her friend's name. She could not see through the fence, because the Germans had packed it with straw. They did not want prisoners to communicate with one another.

"Hanneli," she called, moving down the fence. "Hanneli! It's Anne."

"Here I am," a voice answered. Anne peered into the darkness. Through a chink in the straw she could make out a shadowy figure on the other side of the fence.

"Oh, Anne, what are you doing here?" Hanneli asked. Anne could hear her start to cry. "I thought you were in Switzerland."

Anne began to cry too. "No, that was just a

story we made up to confuse the secret police," Anne told her between sobs. "We were actually hiding close by, in Amsterdam." In bits and pieces, she told her friend all about the Secret Annex, about their Dutch friends and the years of hiding. "But just when we thought we would be saved, the secret police arrested us," she concluded.

All eight were sent to prison camp at Westerbork in northeastern Holland. During the day Anne and her mother and sister worked in the factory taking batteries apart. She could visit with her father and the van Pels. The conditions in the camp were harsh, but bearable. And for the first time in more than two years, Anne could look up into the night sky and see the stars.

"At the end of August we heard the Allies had liberated Paris," she remembered, "and we thought that we would be next."

Instead the Frank family, the van Pelses,

Fritz Pfeffer and more than a thousand others were put on a transport train and shipped to the death camp at Auschwitz, Poland. It was there that the ultimate nightmare began. Immediately the men were separated from the women. Anne had not seen her father since.

"I'm afraid he was sent to the gas chambers," Anne said, trembling. "Every day people were selected for the gas chambers, and we never saw them again."

"Are you sure?" Hanneli said, shocked. "Even the Nazis could not be so evil."

"All day long you could see the smoke rising from the furnaces where the bodies were burned," Anne replied.

From there, Anne and her sister had been sent on to Bergen-Belsen, leaving their mother behind. "Now I have no parents," she said, crying again. "And the strange thing is, the Allies are winning the war. Every time the Germans move us to a new place, the Allied soldiers are right behind."

"Are you sure the Germans are losing?" Hanneli asked.

"Yes, of course they are," Anne replied. "Haven't you heard?"

It turned out that Hanneli had been in Bergen-Belsen for a whole year and knew little of the outside world. Her mother, she told Anne, had died in childbirth shortly after the Franks had disappeared. In June 1943, Hanneli, her father, and her four-year-old sister, Gabi, were rounded up in a *razia*. She, too, had spent time in Westerbork before coming to Bergen-Belsen. But the Goslars were in the "star camp" for people whose names were on a special list. They were supposed to be exchanged for German prisoners of war. Hanneli lived in better conditions than Anne did. Just that day, she had even received a small Red Cross package containing a bit of food.

"If you come back tomorrow night, I will throw the package over the wall to you," she promised Anne. Even though such meetings were dangerous, Anne agreed she would try.

The next night when Anne crept back toward the fence, Hanneli was waiting for her.

"Here I go. Try to catch it," said Hanneli, tossing the package high into the air.

Anne saw something land on the snow nearby. She dashed forward to retrieve it. Yet before she could, a dark shape darted out of the shadows and snatched away her prize.

"No, that's mine!" Anne screamed. She tried to grab the package back, but the person shook her off and ran away. Defeated, Anne collapsed on the ground.

Hanneli had heard what happened through the barbed-wire fence. "Never mind, Anne," she said, trying to comfort her. "I'll try again in a few days."

Two days later bright moonlight flooded the

camp, glinting brightly on the snow. Yet despite the added danger that she would be seen, Hanneli was as good as her word. Again she tossed a packet over the fence, and this time Anne caught it.

Eagerly she tore it open. There were a pair of socks, bread, and some dried fruit. "Oh, thank you, Hanneli," she said. The food could help keep her and Margot alive for another week.

"We'll meet again in a few days," Hanneli promised her. "We will help each other."

"Yes, I will come back," Anne replied. "Good-bye then. See you soon!"

Anne never saw her friend again. A few days later the Frank sisters were moved to another part of Bergen-Belsen. Sometime in late March 1945, Anne and Margot Frank died of typhus. A few weeks later British soldiers liberated the camp.

# CHAPTER FIFTEEN

# ANNE'S LEGACY

It was June 3, 1945, and spring had returned to Amsterdam. From her apartment window Miep could see groups of busy shoppers on the crowded pavement below. On the corner, the vendors were back, selling bright bunches of flowers. A group of children played marbles on a nearby stoop.

Most amazing of all, though, was what she could not see. No Green Police. No German soldiers. No Nazi flags. A month before, on May 7, Germany had surrendered to the Allies. Amsterdam was liberated after a harsh winter in which twenty thousand Dutch men and women perished from starvation and disease.

Now marigolds of bright orange, the royal

color of Holland, bloomed on every vacant lot. Fugitives, pale and nervous, came out of hiding. And refugees began to trickle back home—workers from the forced-labor camps, fugitives from England, Jews and others from the concentration camps.

This warm spring evening Miep was waiting for her husband, Jan, to return from the railroad station. He had gone there to see if he could find out anything about their friends from the Secret Annex. Perhaps one of the returning people had met them in the camps.

Miep leaned farther out the window and peered down the street. That's when she saw him—a tall, thin man, carrying a little parcel. He was heading toward her building.

Before he could knock on the door, she swung it wide open. "Mr. Frank," she said softly to the man on the stoop. "You're back."

"Yes." Otto Frank looked at her for a long moment and cleared his throat. "Edith will not be returning, Miep. But I still have hope for the girls."

Miep felt her eyes fill with tears. She pushed the door wider still. "Come in, Mr. Frank," she said, taking his parcel from him. "This is your home now."

That evening over dinner Otto Frank told Miep and Jan his story. He had not, as Anne had feared, been sent to the gas chambers at Auschwitz. But he had gotten sick. He was in the infirmary when Russian soldiers had marched into the camp on January 27, 1945, and set the prisoners free. Immediately he had gone to the women's barracks to look for his family. That's when he discovered that Edith had died shortly before liberation, and that Margot and Anne had been sent off on a train to another camp far away.

A few days after his return Otto Frank went back to his office at 263 Prinsengracht. He placed ads in newspapers and wrote letters seeking information about his daughters. Finally he received reply. It was from a nurse who had been with Margot and Anne in Bergen-Belsen.

The search was over. His daughters had not survived.

When she heard the news, Miep went to the bottom drawer in her desk. She took out what she had hidden there the day of the arrest.

After the German secret police had left, she and Bep had gone upstairs to the annex. There she had seen Anne's papers and notebooks scattered on the floor. Thinking fast, she had gathered them up, shoved them in her desk drawer, and never looked at them again. Anne's diary was private, Miep thought. It would wait for her until she returned.

Now Miep took the pile of papers into Otto Frank's office. "This is Anne's gift to you," she said simply, placing them on his desk. She went out, softly closing the door behind her.

Otto Frank gazed at the pile in front of him for a long time. Then, hesitantly, he picked up the red and beige diary he had given Anne on her thirteenth birthday. Hardly able to believe what he held in his hands, he opened it up.

"Dearest Kitty," the diary said. He began to read.

From the first page, Otto Frank could tell that he was reading an extraordinary document. He knew that Anne had wanted to turn her diary into a book after the war. Yet many passages in the book were deeply personal. Maybe they were too personal.

Would Anne really have wanted her diary published?

At first he translated passages into German for his mother, who still lived in Switzerland. Next he edited and typed out a complete manuscript, using mostly Anne's revised version of the text. He gave the residents of the annex and their helpers false names, as Anne had planned to do.

Then he started to show the manuscript around. One of the people he gave it to was a famous Dutch historian, Jan Romein. The diary was extraordinary, Romein wrote in a newspaper article. It reminded the world of all it had lost—of the hopes and dreams and talents of millions of young people who had been murdered by the Nazis. The world needed to remember girls like Anne. It needed to make sure this kind of horror never happened again.

Otto Frank had his answer. The voice of his daughter would be heard.

In the months and years to come, Otto Frank discovered the fate of nearly everyone Anne had mentioned in her diary.

Sanne Lederman and Ilse Wagner had both died in the death camps.

Jacqueline van Maarsen, whose mother was French, had been able to get a new identity card as a non-Jew. She remained in Amsterdam and later raised a family.

Hello Silberberg had crossed the border to Belgium to be with his parents, who had escaped from Germany. After the war he emigrated to the United States and settled in New Jersey.

Hermann van Pels had died in the gas chamber at Auschwitz. His wife, Auguste, had accompanied the Frank girls to Bergen-Belsen. From there she'd been transported to two other camps, and died sometime during the spring of 1945. Her son, Peter, had helped care for Otto Frank at Auschwitz. But Peter was forced out of the camp on a death march in mid-January. He died on May 5, two days before the Germans surrendered.

Johannes Kleiman and Victor Kugler, who were also arrested in the raid on the Secret Annex, had been sent to labor camps. They survived and came back to work for Mr. Frank.

For years no word came of Fritz Pfeffer. Finally Otto Frank found out that he, too, had died, in a concentration camp in northern Germany.

A month after he first read Anne's diary, her father took a train to the nearby city of Maastricht. There he visited a hospital where a dear friend was staying.

"Mr. Frank!" Hanneli Goslar exclaimed when he walked into her room. She was so surprised and glad to see him. "Where is Anne?" she asked.

Quietly he told her that Anne had not made it.

"I saw Anne at Bergen-Belsen," Hanneli said sadly. She told him about her last few desperate meetings with Anne. "We promised to meet again, Mr. Frank. But then my father died. When I returned to the fence a few days later, her section of the camp had been moved."

Hanneli and her sister, Gabi, were the only members of her family to survive. Because Hanneli had tuberculosis, she was recovering in a hospital, and Gabi was in a nearby orphanage. But soon they would be together again.

From then on, Otto Frank became almost like a father to the orphaned girls. He brought them to Switzerland, where Hanneli could receive the care she needed. He kept in close contact when they emigrated to Palestine. Hanneli became a nurse—just as Margot Frank had hoped to do. She was in Jerusalem when Israel became a Jewish nation in 1948. There she married and had three children and eventually, ten grandchildren.

One night in Jerusalem Hanneli went to a play about a Jewish girl hiding out in Amsterdam during World War II. When the lights came back on, the audience stood up and applauded her. They knew she had been Anne Frank's childhood companion in real life. And by then Hanneli's old friend was known throughout the world.

Anne's book was published in Holland in 1947, under the name she had chosen: *Het Achterhuis*. At first sales were slow, but then its popularity grew. After being published in America in 1952 as *The Diary of a Young Girl,* it was suddenly enormously successful. A play based on the book was written and performed, and then a movie was made based on the play. Altogether, since its original publication, Anne's diary has been translated into sixty languages and read by tens of millions of people around the globe. Just as Anne wished, she has become a famous writer—a *very* famous writer.

One mystery has remained. Who betrayed Anne and the others to the secret police? In 1948, the Dutch police opened an investigation. At first suspicion fell on an Opekta warehouse supervisor. But the police had no solid proof, and he was never accused. Later Melissa Muller, Anne's biographer, suggested that the betrayer may have been the wife of another warehouse worker. A biographer of Otto Frank suggested that the culprit was a pro-Nazi acquaintance of Mr. Frank. The police investigated these accusations but uncovered no convincing evidence. The mystery has never been solved.

Otto Frank devoted the rest of his life to preserving his daughter's memory. He led the drive to save 263 Prinsengracht from demolition and opened it as a museum in 1960. Today nearly one million visitors come to the Anne Frank House each year to learn about Anne Frank's life and explore the Secret Annex where she wrote her diary. Otto Frank also established a foundation to promote peace and understanding among young people around the world.

Readers of the diary continue to fall in love

with Anne. They admire her courage, laugh at her humor, and sympathize with her conflicts with her parents. Her idealism tempered—but not destroyed—by persecution and war, continues to inspire others. Because of her diary, Anne's spirit lives on.

On June 12, 2004, the Anne Frank House celebrated the seventy-fifth anniversary of Anne's birth. Ninety-five-year-old Miep Gies opened the celebration. Visiting children watched a showing of *The Lighthouse Keeper*—the Rin Tin Tin movie Anne showed at her thirteenth birthday party so long ago.

A newspaper reporter asked Miep what Anne would have become if she had lived. "Oh, a writer of course," Miep answered. "A good, famous writer . . . and a grandmother. She would have been a grandmother."

# AFTERWORD

As the Allied armies swept across Europe in the winter and spring of 1945, they uncovered the largest and most horrifying murder plot in the history of the world. In small towns in Germany, Poland, Czechoslovakia, and Austria soldiers stumbled across camps filled with stacks of corpses and barracks filled with skeletal, hollow-eyed prisoners. The concentration camps that Anne and her friends had so feared were not only real, they were worse than anyone could possibly have imagined. As the first images of emaciated victims and gas ovens appeared in newspapers and newsreels, a horror-struck world began to understand what Hitler and the Nazis had done. Supreme Allied

Commander Dwight D. Eisenhower, whose troops liberated the concentration camp Ohrdruf, made sure that his soldiers toured the camp. Now, he said, they would know what they had been fighting against.

The death of Anne Frank was one small incident in what is now called the Holocaust, the planned persecution and killing of European Jews by the Nazi regime. In 1933, when Hitler came to power, approximately 9 million Jews lived in Europe. By 1945, 6 million of them had been murdered. The "Final Solution," as the Nazi plan to annihilate the Jews was called, was planned with brutal efficiency. Between 1942 and 1945, Jewish people throughout occupied Europe were transported by railway to specialized death camps, where they were killed in chambers filled with poison gas and their bodies burned. On September 3, 1944, Anne Frank and her family were among the 1,019 prisoners on the last transport from

Westerbork to the death camp at Auschwitz. Of these, 45 men and 82 women survived the war.

As Allied armies neared and the Germans realized they were losing the war, the killings were speeded up. SS guards transported prisoners to other camps or sent them on "death marches" to keep them from being liberated.

The Nazis murdered nearly 6 million other people too. Some, like artists, writers, religious leaders, and Communists, were political prisoners. Most of these people died in concentration or forced-labor camps as a result of mistreatment, hunger, and disease. Others, like the Roma (Gypsies), Russian prisoners of war, homosexuals, or the mentally and physically handicapped were killed because the Nazis considered them inferior. Tens of thousands of Roma were gassed to death. According to an eyewitness, at Auschwitz Anne Frank saw a group of Gypsy children on their way to the gas chambers and began to cry. "Oh, look at their eyes," she murmured.

Anne Frank has become a symbol of the 1.5 million children murdered by the Nazis in the concentration camps of World War II. Like Anne, each one of these children was an individual with friends and family, hopes, fears, and plans for the future. In the story of Anne Frank we can glimpse the fate of all the others, and understand what was lost when they died.

# FOR FURTHER READING

## ABOUT ANNE FRANK:

Frank, Anne. *Anne Frank's Tales from the Secret Annex.* New York: Bantam, 1994.

★ ———. *The Diary of a Young Girl: The Definitive Edition.* Edited by Otto H. Frank and Mirjam Pressler. New York: Doubleday, 1995.

★ Gies, Miep, with Alison Leslie Gold. *Anne Frank Remembered: The Story of the Woman Who Helped to Hide the Frank Family.* New York: Simon & Schuster, 1987.

Gold, Alison Leslie. *Memories of Anne Frank: Reflections of a Childhood Friend.* New York: Scholastic, 1997. The experiences of Hannah Pick-Goslar (Hanneli) during World War II.

Metselaar, Menno, Ruud van der Rol, and
Dineke Stam, compilation and editing.
*Anne Frank House: A Museum with a Story.*
Amsterdam: Anne Frank House, 1999.

Pressler, Mirjam. *Anne Frank: A Hidden Life.*
New York: Dutton, 1999.

Rubin, Susan Goldman. *Searching for Anne
Frank: Letters from Amsterdam to Iowa.* New
York: Abrams, 2003. The parallel stories of
Anne and Margot Frank and the sisters in
Iowa who were their pen pals.

Van der Rol, Ruud, and Rian Verhoeven for
the Anne Frank House. *Anne Frank: Beyond
the Diary.* New York: Viking, 1993. A photo-
graphic remembrance.

# ABOUT THE HOLOCAUST

Greenfeld, Howard. *The Hidden Children*. Boston: Houghton Mifflin, 1997. Real-life stories of Jewish children who survived the Holocaust in hiding.

* Meltzer, Milton. *Never to Forget: The Jews of the Holocaust*. New York: Dell, 1977.

Pettit, Jayne. *A Place to Hide: True Stories of Holocaust Rescues*. New York: Scholastic, 1997. True stories of the rescue of Jews during the Holocaust.

* Rogasky, Barbara. *Smoke and Ashes: The Story of the Holocaust*. New York: Holiday House, 2002

Rossel, Seymour. *The Holocaust: The Fire That Raged*. New York: Franklin Watts, 1990.

# FICTION ABOUT THE HOLOCAUST

* Isaacs, Anne. *Torn Thread*. New York: Scholastic, 2000. Two Polish-Jewish girls try to survive in a labor camp in Czechoslovakia during World War II.

Kerr, Judith. *When Hitler Stole Pink Rabbit*. New York: Paperstar, 1997. A nine-year-old Jewish girl and her family travel from Germany to England in the early 1930s.

Lowry, Lois. *Number the Stars*. Boston: Houghton Mifflin, 1989. A Danish girl helps her family hide some Jewish friends from the Nazis.

* Perl, Lila. *Four Perfect Pebbles: A Holocaust Story*. New York: HarperTrophy, 1999. A true story of a Jewish family's journey from Germany to Holland and then to Bergen-Belsen.

Reiss, Johanna. *The Upstairs Room.* New York: HarperTrophy, 1972. A ten-year-old Dutch-Jewish girl and her sister hide in the upstairs room of a peasant's home during the Nazi occupation.

Vos, Ida. *Anna Is Still Here.* New York: Puffin Books, 1995. A child who was hidden during the war struggles to adjust to freedom in Holland.

Vos, Ida. *Hide and Seek.* Boston: Houghton Mifflin, 1990. A Jewish girl grows up in Nazi-occupied Holland.

# VIDEOS AND CD-ROMS

* *Anne Frank: The Whole Story.* Directed by Robert Dornhel. Buena Vista Home Entertainment, 2001. The story of Anne's life before, during, and after her time in hiding. Based on *Anne Frank: The Biography* by Melissa Müller.

* *Anne Frank Remembered.* A Jon Blair Film Company Production. Columbia Tristar Home Entertainment, 1995. Contains interviews with people who knew Anne, including Miep Gies and Hanneli Pick-Goslar.

*Biography: Anne Frank—The Life of a Young Girl.* A & E Entertainment, 1999.

*The Diary of Anne Frank.* Directed by George Stevens. Twentieth Century Fox, 1959. The movie based on the play about Anne in hiding.

*Remembering Anne Frank,* with Miep Gies. CD-ROM. Anne Frank House, 1998.

# WEB SITES

Anne Frank Center, New York
www.annefrank.com

Anne Frank House
www.annefrank.org

Simon Wiesenthal Center
www.wiesenthal.com

United States Holocaust Memorial Museum
www.ushmm.org

\* For older children